Your Towns and Cities in the G

Exeter
in the Great War

Your Towns and Cities in the Great War

Exeter
in the Great War

Derek Tait

Pen & Sword
MILITARY

First published in Great Britain in 2015 by
PEN & SWORD MILITARY
an imprint of
Pen and Sword Books Ltd
47 Church Street
Barnsley
South Yorkshire S70 2AS

ISBN 978 1 47382 309 9

A CIP record for this book is available from the British Library

Printed and bound in England
by CPI Group (UK) Ltd, Croydon, CR0 4YY

Pen & Sword Books Ltd incorporates the imprints of
Pen & Sword Archaeology, Atlas, Aviation, Battleground, Discovery,
Family History, History, Maritime, Military, Naval, Politics, Railways,
Select, Social History, Transport, True Crime, and Claymore Press,
Frontline Books, Leo Cooper, Praetorian Press, Remember When,
Seaforth Publishing and Wharncliffe.

For a complete list of Pen and Sword titles please contact
Pen and Sword Books Limited
47 Church Street, Barnsley, South Yorkshire, S70 2AS, England
E-mail: enquiries@pen-and-sword.co.uk
Website: www.pen-and-sword.co.uk

Contents

Acknowledgements   6

1914 – Eagar for a fight   7

1915 – Deepening conflict   47

1916 – The realization   73

1917 – Seeing it through   95

1918 – The final blows   117

Bibliography   141
Index   143

Acknowledgements

Thanks to David Cornforth and John Roberts for extra photos supplied. Thanks also to Tina Cole and Tilly Barker.

CHAPTER ONE

1914 – Eager for a Fight

Rising tensions in Europe and the assassination of Franz Ferdinand in Sarajevo led to Austria-Hungary's declaration of war on Serbia. This led to the Central Powers, which included Germany and Austria-Hungary, and the Allies, which included the British Empire, the French Republic and the Russian Empire, declaring war on each other, which led to the commencement of the First World War on 28 July 1914.

The *Western Times* of 30 July carried the following news:

Mr W.R. Mallett of Exwick Mills, Exeter, informs us that during a conversation he had by telephone with the Baltic Exchange, London, he was informed that rumours were current between 3 and 4 o'clock yesterday that Russia had declared war on Austria. A telegram, through Reuter, from Paris, however, tends to discount the rumours and to indicate a probable easing of the situation.

The *Exeter and Plymouth Gazette* of Friday 31 July announced:

Owing to extreme pressure on our space today, caused by a very large number of advertisements, important war news and a number of local events of interest,

Archduke Franz Ferdinand of Austria. Ferdinand's assassination in Sarajevo on 28 June 1914 lead to Austria-Hungary's declaration of war on Serbia, which ultimately led to the beginning of the First World War.

several reports have had to be necessarily much curtailed and others are held over.

Also on the 31 July the *Western Times* reported:

It had been planned that the 7th Devons, who are encamped at Churston, should pay a visit to Exeter today, the Mayor having consented to officially welcoming them. Yesterday morning, the officer commanding informed his Worship by telegram that the visit had been unavoidably cancelled.

On 4 August, Britain declared war on Germany. This followed an 'unsatisfactory reply' to the British ultimatum that Belgium should remain neutral.

On the day that war was declared The *Flying Post* reported:

Scenes of enthusiasm which were witnessed on Tuesday, when the Devon and Cornwall Brigade of Territorials marched from their camp at Woodbury into Exeter continued until late evening. The 4th Devons, in which citizens were naturally most interested, were the last to arrive about nine in the night, and as they passed through the streets on the way to St David's Station they were cheered by the thousands of citizens. There was a remarkable scene at St David's, a great crowd cheering the men, the King, and the French nation,

People of the city gathering outside the Exeter and Plymouth Gazette *offices on 6 August 1914 to read the latest news of the war.*

finally singing the National Anthem and 'Rule Britannia'. Another
burst of enthusiasm in the High Street greeted the news of the
declaration of war against Germany.

On 6 August, the *North Devon Journal* reported that the 6th Devons, who had been camped at Woodbury, were to be moved to Plymouth after a despatch order had been received. The order had called for their immediate removal to Barnstable but the order was changed and they were told to make their way to Plymouth. Special trains carried them from Exeter to Plymouth. They proceeded to the Drill Hall at Millbay, where arrangements had been made to billet the men.

The *Western Times* of Friday 7 August reported that an important duty within the city was the guarding of railway bridges and tunnels. It was noted that there were several German citizens settled in Exeter and that although these citizens are known to the police and may have 'no evil intentions', their presence makes it necessary to take the utmost precautions. As in the Boer War, the guarding of bridges and tunnels fell under the jurisdiction of the police, who were armed for the purpose. The work caused a great strain on the Exeter Police Force, of whom at least a dozen men, being members of the Army Reserve, had to return to the colours. Many constables were working eighteen-hour shifts to guard the bridges and it was suggested that some of this work

Horses of the Royal Field Artillery en route to the station on 6 August 1914. There
was a great demand for horses at the front throughout the war and many were
requisitioned from local farmers, etc.

could be undertaken by members of the National Reserve. The suggestion met with approval from the chief constable as well as from Councillor W. Brock, who issued notices inviting men from the National Reserve willing to undertake this duty to report to his establishment at Fore Street.

Within half-an-hour of the notices being posted, more than twenty men applied to help. One man said he had his own double-barrelled gun and would arm himself with it whenever he was called upon to guard.

The paper continued:

> The National Reserve men will undertake duty for an hour or two at a time at hours which will not interfere with their ordinary employment. Some of them intimated that they were available for any time of the day or night.
>
> A number of recruits were enrolled in the City Police Force yesterday for temporary duty during the absence of the Reserve Men at the front.

Major St Maur, the Liberal candidate for Exeter, wrote to Mr Munro (his agent) saying:

> It looks very much as if I shall be mobilised with my Yeomanry in a

The Devon Reserves, nearly 900 strong, on a route march through Exeter on 7 August 1914. They are shown parading along Sidwell Street. Members of the brass section of the company played as the soldiers marched as locals, including children, turned out to watch.

day or two, and, in that event I should be moving to another part of the country, and this will prevent my undertaking any political engagements, or taking part in the political campaign for some time to come. The only hope I can see at present is that the awfulness of the war now undertaken may cause it to be of short duration. Should this hope prove correct, I shall look forward to starting the campaign at the earliest possible moment.

Major St Maur was part of the 1st Royal Devon Yeomanry Cavalry, which was stationed at temporary premises at Southernhay while awaiting mobilisation.

On the morning of Friday 7 August, the Army Reservists stationed at Higher Barracks, Exeter, who numbered 900 men, marched through the city in the hope of encouraging new recruits to enlist with the colours. The men marched from the barracks at 10am and proceeded by way of York Road to Old Tiverton Road, Mount Pleasant, down Mount Bath Road and straight through the city to Bonhay Road before returning to the barracks.

The railways were soon brought under government control using the Regulation of Forces act of 1871. Farm wagons and steam lorries from

A parade of Devon Reserves in Exeter on 7 August 1914, passing by London Inn Square and Eastgate. Many onlookers turned out to cheer them on.

An appeal to help the Prince of Wales National Relief Fund. On Saturday 8 August 1914, The Mayor of Exeter (Mr W Kendall King) received a telegram from HRH The Prince of Wales. It read: 'Earnestly trust that you will assist my National Relief Fund by opening subscription list without delay and forward results to Buckingham Palace. Please do all that lies in your power to interest those among whom your influence extends. (Signed) Edward P.'

The smiling faces of the Devon Reserves standing at ease on 7 August 1914.

the city's brewery were requisitioned by the military to provide transport for the Territorials.

Horses were also required for the war effort and owners were requested to take them to a field near Higher Barracks, where they were inspected by local vets and remount officers. Suitable animals were bought immediately.

On 8 August, the 3rd (Reserve) Battalion of the Devonshire Regiment moved from Exeter to Plymouth.

The *Western Times* of 11 August noted that there appeared to be no panic buying of food at the Higher Market on the previous Friday. Shoppers found an excellent supply of butter, cream, eggs and poultry, which was supplied by local farmers. However, eggs were up to 1½d

Part of Kitchener's New Army at Exeter. The men shown were recruited at Cardiff and the sign attached to the table reads: 'Cardiff City Knuts.'

Kitchener's New Army at Exeter's football ground. The new recruits are shown smiling and waving their caps.

each and butter was 1s. 4d a lb. Ducks were 2s. 6d each. There was a shortage of beef at Exeter cattle market due to animals no longer being brought to the city by rail.

The paper went on to say:

*The **Exeter and Plymouth Gazette** of Saturday 15 August 1914 carried a picture of the RAMC (Wessex Field Ambulance) marching through Exeter as they prepared to leave the city.*

It speaks volumes for the admirable organisation of the country's food supplies, and the calm courage and sangfroid of the fishermen, who must have been pursuing their avocations right up to and during the sea troubles, that there is no shortage to record as yet in the fish market, and that prices so far have not been inflated. Hake is dearer but that is, we are informed, owing to a natural shortage only, most of the hake supply coming from the neighbourhood of Milford Haven which is out of the war zone.

An announcement in the *Exeter and Plymouth Gazette* of Tuesday 11 August read:

The War.
As a result, many situations are vacant and labour is required.
'Too old at forty' does not apply now.
Persons seeking employment should send their advertisements to the Gazette, the best paper in the West.

The RAMC (Wessex Field Ambulance) leaving Exeter by train as reported in the **Exeter and Plymouth Gazette** *of Saturday 15 August 1914. The troops smile and wave at the many onlookers who have come to cheer them on.*

The Devons leaving Queen Street Station, Exeter, on the morning of Thursday 20 August 1914. Many are hanging out of the windows of the carriages waving goodbye to onlookers.

On 18 August, the mayor, Mr W. Kendall King, presided over a meeting at the Guildhall. Its aim was to further recruitment for the second army. The mayor announced that a leaflet had been printed stating the physical requirements of applicants as well as rates of pay. There was much deliberation over how the procedure for recruiting should take place with a Mr Stooker saying if there was insufficient response then compulsory enlistment would have to be enforced.

On Wednesday 19 August, the *Exeter and Plymouth Gazette* reported that thirty German prisoners from Dartmouth and South Devon had been brought to Exeter the previous day. In the same article it was reported that the finance sub-committee of the Exeter War Relief Committee announced that the total amount of money raised to date for the Exeter National Relief Fund (Prince of Wales's appeal) was £1,264 7s.

The first shots by British troops on foreign soil took place on 21 August 1914. A military unit of the 4th Dragoon Guards, comprising 120 men, was sent on a reconnoitre mission ahead of the British Expeditionary Force. Although members of the British Expeditionary Force had landed a week before, no contact with the enemy had taken place. As forces advanced into France and Belgium, they heard stories from civilians that large numbers of German troops were advancing towards the town of Mons in Belgium. Shortly after, the cavalry men of the Dragoon Guards encountered the enemy, and the first shots taken

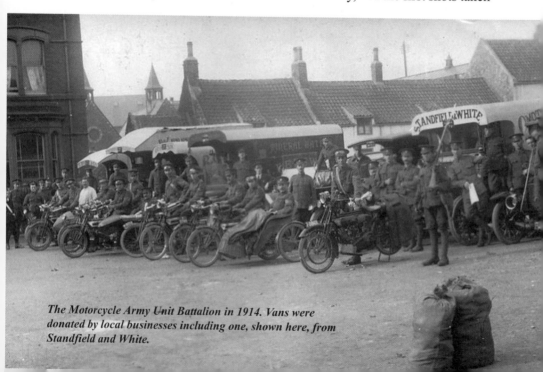

The Motorcycle Army Unit Battalion in 1914. Vans were donated by local businesses including one, shown here, from Standfield and White.

in Europe since the Battle of Waterloo became the first of millions to be fired over the next four years.

On the evening of Tuesday 25 August, the second of a series of patriotic concerts was held at Northernhay and drew a large audience. The Salvation Army silver band proved very popular and vocal numbers were provided by Mr Arthur Kellet, who was a tenor at St Paul's Cathedral, and Mr Frederic James, who was a baritone gold medallist. The next concert was announced for the following Saturday with the Exeter Male Voice Choir together with Pipe-Major Johnstone taking part in sword dances and the Highland fling. The proceeds from the concerts were contributed to the War Fund.

On 28 August, the *Western Times* reported:

Several recruits presented themselves for acceptance at Exeter again yesterday. These were mainly dealt with at the Higher Barracks and the majority were passed. The number was not so large as in the earlier part of the week but this was only to be expected, and really Exeter and the district have made a very creditable response to the call to arms, while it was clearly shown at the St. Thomas meeting on Wednesday that the source of supply is by no means exhausted.

About a dozen or fourteen of the local body of National Reserve have already joined the Kitchener Army. The rest of the National Reservists are anxious to render help to the country in some form or other at this time, and they feel somewhat aggrieved that their service is not being called for by the military authorities. There are in the immediate vicinity quite 400 of these Reservists, and many of them have had active service, while all, of course, have undergone military training. Surely there are many ways in which such a body of men could be of material assistance. Their training, too, might be facilitated if the authorities would grant them the use of the Territorial Drill Halls, rifle ranges, etc. The men were called out for drill in the Castle Yard Wednesday and a subsequent route march. They were under command of Major Biddell, the local hon. secretary; Captains Birkett, Drew and W. Brock. Another parade will be held tomorrow.

The article continued with a report about food prices within Exeter. It read:

Food prices in Exeter are, it is good news to learn, practically down to the normal again. There are one or two exceptions, as for instance, sugar, which is still slightly inflated in value; but generally speaking prices have settled down to almost what they were before the war started. This may not be acceptable reading to those well-to-do ladies and gentlemen who exhibited such fine patriotism and consideration for their poorer neighbours by grabbing all the necessities they could lay their hands on when they thought there was a likelihood of a shortage and a consequent jump in prices; but it will be welcome intelligence to the toilers and the moilers, and the wives and children of those who have gone into the fighting line, and, perhaps, all the more so in that the grabbers are now biting their fingers at their foolish precipitation. Supplies are coming along pretty regularly, though perhaps, delivery is not quite so prompt as

The War Book of Facts was available from the **Western Times** *of Monday 31 August 1914. The book was packed with information and was said to tell the reader everything he wanted to know about the war.*

before the outbreak of hostilities. But with the ordinary train service now being resumed, business will be able to proceed with very little trouble or delay.

THE FIELD OF——FOOTBALL

THE Exeter City Association Football Club, in common with other Professional Teams, intend carrying out their programme during the present season.

What encouragement will the heroes who are shedding their life's blood on the battlefield derive when they learn that the men at home are laughing and shouting on the football field ?

Dare we tell our Colonial brothers that while they are sacrificing their homes and their country to fight for the old flag, we are watching football ?

What mockery, should the cheers and shouts from the football crowd reach the ears of the mothers and sisters whose dear ones have fallen on the battlefield!

I Germany playing any other game but war ?

Could a mob of youths and men be found in Belgium to-day shouting themselves hoarse over football ?

Are the French or Russians wasting their time, or watching anything less than the movement of the common enemy ?

What the country wants is soldiers, and not what Kipling has so well described as " muddied oofs."

An advert in the **Exeter and Plymouth Gazette** *of Thursday 3 September 1914 objecting to the continuation of professional football while the war is on.*

On 31 August the *Western Times* and the *Express and Echo* offered the War Book of Facts for 2/9. Within its pages were eighteen chapters, 3,000 facts and figures and a special map telling the reader all he wanted to know about the war.

The *Western Times* of Thursday 3 September reported on the clothing and money that was being provided for homeless Belgians. The article read:

That it is scarcely possible to exaggerate the destitute condition of the Belgian refugees flocking to London is shown by an extract from a private letter just received in Exeter. In this it is definitely stated that so hurried was the flight of these brave, devoted people, including women, children, old and invalided men, that some of the babies were actually brought over to our Metropolis wrapped round with newspapers. There had been no time to dress them or secure their clothes.

The Mayoress of Exeter's fund for garments and funds for the Belgians has already met with a generous response and on Tuesday, Miss Andrew, who has undertaken this department, sent two large bales of most useful articles for the refugees to the Belgian Legation in London. Many of these represented real sacrifice on the part of the donors. One, writing over the initials, 'T.M.B.', in sending a nice costume said, 'I wish I could give something of more value but I've only three dresses to my name. Still I can spare this if it is of any good to some poor Belgian girl or woman.' A subscription of two

Fresh recruits for Kitchener's New Army. On Saturday 5 September 1914, the Western Times *reported:* **'Yesterday there was another large influx of troops at the Exeter High Barracks. Neither in number or quality is there any decline. Thursday, the six counties, of which Exeter is in the centre, raised a further 1,187 men and Devon took second place on the list.' The recruits are shown in Church Road, St Thomas, after enlisting at the County Ground.**

The **Devon and Exeter Gazette** *of Saturday 5 September 1914 carried a picture under the headline 'For King and country'. The caption read: 'A detachment of troops who left Exeter, yesterday morning, to join the 4th Battalion Devon Regiment (TF), which has volunteered for foreign service. They have expressed their readiness to 'go anywhere' and include five members of the Gazette staff.'*

shillings was also received from the wife of a private in the Devons and other sums brought the fund up to about £10 yesterday. Further sums and goods are urgently needed and should be sent to Miss Andrew, c/o Messrs. J. Hinton Lake and Son, 41 High Street, Exeter. A lady, by the way, is generously giving her child's brown 'Millson' crib for the use of a Belgian baby. The cot is complete with all bedding but, the mattress being previously given away, another is needed, if anyone has one for which they have no further use.

On Saturday 5 September, many recruits left the city to join the ranks and were seen off at the station by the mayoress and ladies of the committee of the Hospitality Fund. Each soldier was presented with a large sausage roll, two pieces of cake, two bananas, two apples and some cigarettes. The small gifts were much appreciated by the soldiers. The mayoress thanked the poorer people of Exeter who had contributed to the fund with a number of sixpences and other small coins donated to the committee by people living in Coombe Street, Rack Street, and other poor localities within the city.

In the *Devon and Exeter Gazette* of Saturday 5 September, a cartoon appeared with the caption 'Rifle or Football – which?'. There was a growing feeling that football shouldn't continue while the war was on.

Lord Roberts said it would be disgraceful if the sport continued and the newspaper agreed with him.

The *Western Times* of Monday 7 September reported:

Further contingents of recruits presented themselves to the military

Rifle or Football——Which?

While the players of Exeter City and West Ham are charging each other at St. James's Park, this afternoon, Britain's brave sons will be charging the Germans on a foreign soil. While those who attend the match are cheering the manœuvring of a leather ball, hundreds and thousands of mothers, wives, sisters, & children, will be sitting, hoping against hope, that they may not receive the message which tells them that never again in this world will they see those nearest and dearest to them, they having fallen victims to a ball of lead. Lord Roberts recently said it would be disgraceful if football was continued during the war. We agree with him. So far as the Football Association is concerned, it is simply a question of gate-money, and their paltry contribution of £1,250 to the National Relief Fund deceives nobody.

*A notice in the **Devon and Exeter Gazette** of Saturday 5 September 1914 carried the headline 'Rifle or football'. The newspaper said that it would be disgraceful if football continued during the war and Lord Roberts called for it to be stopped.*

authorities in the city on Saturday and the steady flow of young men passing from civil to military active life continues with no sign, as yet, of diminution.

The *Exeter and Plymouth Gazette* of 7 September reported that the number of articles sent to the Linen League by the Mayoress of Exeter (Mrs W. Kendall King) and her working party had reached 4,587 items. Large parcels had been sent to Belgian refugees and direct to soldiers at the front. The headquarters of the party had been transferred from the Guildhall to the premises next door, formerly occupied by the Domestic Bazaar Company. The party, with the mayoress in charge, were actively engaged in receiving clothing and 'comforts' on behalf

On Monday 7 September 1914, the Exeter and Devon Gazette *published a photo of men enjoying a football match under the headline 'More Men are Needed'. The caption read: 'The above photograph was taken during the progress of the Southern League football match between Exeter City and West Ham, at St James' Park on Saturday, and shows that with some people there is little thought for those who are giving their lives for King and country when a lad imported from the North of England scores a goal for the 'Ever Faithful!' Some of the young fellows who found themselves next to gentlemen in khaki must have felt heartily ashamed of themselves – provided, of course, they retain any self respect. Our advice to the latter is to cut out the above photograph, preserve it, and hand it down to those who are to come after them in remembrance of what they did when Britain was at war with Germany in 1914.*

of the Devon Voluntary Aid Organisation and Linen League. The mayoress and ladies helping her had also been active in the previous week, meeting the troop trains at the stations and handing out food, fruit and cigarettes, etc.

On 17 September, the *Exeter and Plymouth Gazette* mentioned that they had received a letter from a detachment of Marines who had passed through Exeter after leaving Plymouth. The letter said they would like to thank the Mayoress of Exeter and the people who passed them gifts on their way through the station. They were quoted as saying 'the little packages were most acceptable'.

On Monday 21 September, the *Exeter and Plymouth Gazette* reported on the suicide of an ex-NCO. The story read:

> *Exonians heard with deep regret yesterday that ex-Quartermaster-Sergeant Dyer, late of the Devon Regiment, had been found dead under tragic circumstances at his residence in Mount Pleasant Road, Exeter, about 5 o'clock that morning. The sad discovery was made by Mrs Dyer who found her husband, in his night attire, lying on the floor of the kitchen with his throat cut and apparently dead. Dr Bradford was called but could only pronounce life extinct and the body was removed to the mortuary to await the inquest which will be heard later today.*

The HM Transport Nevasa, which carried the 4th and 5th Battalion of the Devon Regiment (the Territorials), also known as the 'Devon Terriers', overseas.

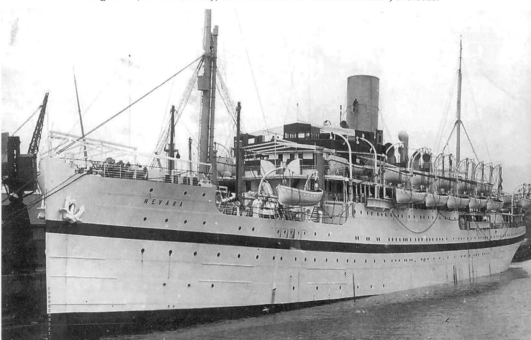

The deceased, who was extremely popular, especially among the Devons, had been engaged at the barracks lately and it is suggested that he overtaxed his strength. Q.M.S. Dyer suffered a severe shock several years ago when his son went down with the Titanic. Another son has recently enlisted in Kitchener's Army. Deceased was 58 years of age.

The *Western Times* of 24 September reported that the Sir Francis Drake bowls team from Plymouth had beaten Barnstaple in the Devon Rink Competition at Exeter. The score was 23-15.

The *Western Times* of 26 September reported the deaths of two army officers from Exeter, Major H. T. Wynter and Lieutenant Wissman of the Royal Field Artillery. Both officers were said to be well-known and the newspaper reported that their deaths would be met with much sorrow in the city. Major Wynter had formerly been an adjutant to the Wessex Division of the Royal Field Artillery (Territotials), which was commanded by Colonel Talbot. He resided at The Elms, Wonford, was very popular and was a talented amateur actor in annual productions of musical comedy at Exeter Theatre, taking leading roles in *Veronique* and *The Girl From Kays*.

PC Townhill, a former member of the Exeter police force, was enrolled in the Royal Field Artillery and was stationed at Topsham Barracks. At the outbreak of the war he returned as a reserve to the colours and, as a member of the 29th Battery RFA, he proceeded with the 42nd Brigade of the British Expeditionary Force to France. His name later appeared in the dispatches from Field Marshal Sir John French.

In the *Exeter and Plymouth Gazette* of Saturday 3 October 1914, letters were published from soldiers thanking people for sending them gifts after an appeal by Exeter's mayoress. The gifts included blankets, shirts, socks and other useful items. On the previous day, the mayoress had received a postcard from a soldier addressed to her at the Guildhall. It read:

The box of soldiers' comforts from you which reached this hospital was greatly appreciated, and I send you my warmest thanks for it. S.F. Clark, Lieut-Col. R.A.M.C. Commanding No 3 General Hospital.

In the same mail, the Mayoress also received a letter from a Major Anstey who was serving with the 4th Devons. It read:

My Dear Mayoress,

Ever so many thanks for the belts which have been given out to the men. They are delighted to have them.

I am so very much obliged to you, also, for taking so much trouble in getting us some books and games.

Please tell all your kind helpers how very grateful we are for all their goodness to us. We shall try to be a credit to them abroad.

Yours sincerely,
Alfred Anstey.

The final letter published, stated what the rank and file thought of the gifts. It read:

B Co., 4th Batt. Devon Regt. 30th Sept. 1914.

To the Mayoress.

Madam,

Received cardigan jacket quite safe and return you my very best thanks. I appreciate your kindness very much and don't think you will ever regret taking so much trouble for our soldiers – Regulars and Territorials.

Yours faithfully,
(Pte) C. Crocker.

The Territorials leaving Torrington for foreign shores, as published in the Exeter and Plymouth Gazette of Tuesday 6 October 1914. Well-wishers, who have come to see them off, can also be seen in the photo.

Meanwhile, entertainment carried on in Exeter. In the same newspaper, further down the page, was news of a forthcoming event the following week at the Theatre Royal. The play *Mary Goes First,* which had just finished a successful six-month run at London's Playhouse Theatre, was due to run for three nights and was described as the 'most amusing comedy full of clever lines and amusing situations'.

On 4 October, The West of England Eye Hospital was mobilised and became VA

...orials leaving Barnstaple Station for foreign ...e. The photo appeared in the **Exeter and Plymouth ...tte** *of Tuesday 6 October 1914 and shows them ...g to friends, relatives and well-wishers.*

Hospital No 1. It was the first of seven military hospitals in the area, the others being VA No 2 The Modern School at Bishop Blackall, VA No 3 The City Hospital at Heavitree, VA No 4 at Topsham Barracks, VA No 5 The College Hostel at Bradninch House, VA No 6 Bishop's Palace and VA No 7 at the Streatham Hall Temporary Hospital.

...he Modern School in Exeter, which ...ecame Temporary Hospital No 2 during ...e war. VA hospitals around the city ...ecame vital for the treatment of ...ounded troops returning to England.

The Modern School, Exeter (Temporary Hospital, No 2)   Chandler's Series

The Royal First Devon Yeomanry as they appeared in the Devon and Exeter Gazette of Friday 9 October 1914. The men, who were training at Exeter, are shown with their honorary colonel, Sir John Shelley.

During October 1914, Mrs Jackman of 37 Portland Street received an intimation from the War Office that her son, Percy (shown left), had been killed in action. He was a private in the 3rd Battalion Coldstream Guards. He had spent seven years with his regiment, two of them in Egypt.

The Western Times of Friday 9 October carried the story of the death of a young soldier. It read:

Exonian killed by the bayonet.

Mr F W Bridle of Sandford Street, Exeter has been notified by the War Office of the fact that his son, Pte Frederick William Bridle, of the D.C.L.I., died on September 10th as the result of a bayonet thrust sustained at the Front. Deceased, who was well-known in the City, joined the Army just under three years ago.

On the same day, the *Western Times* told of an Exonian's 'thrilling adventures at the Front'. Sapper Harry Clift had been a telegraphist at the Exeter Post Office when he was called up at the beginning of the war as a reservist with the Royal Engineers. Sapper Clift had previously fought in the Boer War and had returned home 'without a scratch'. He was said to have many friends in Exeter particularly amongst the city's football club's followers.

*The **Western Times** of Friday 9 October 1914 announced the death of Drummer Kilgannon of the Devonshire Regiment. He died in hospital as the result of wounds. He was well-known in Exeter and was regularly seen playing in military processions in the city. He left a wife and four children.*

Lieutenant W. T. Gill appeared in the **Devon and Exeter Gazette** *in October 1914 after being awarded the Legion of Honour by the French Government. Lieutenant Gill, of the 6th Dragoon Guards, and a corporal, together with thirty men, held a bridge for several hours against 500 Germans. He was the cousin of Mrs Charles Seymour of Blackall Road, Exeter.*

From a diary he kept, he wrote a letter home which detailed his experiences at the Front. Part of it read:

I regret that I am not allowed to mention the name of any particular spot but will give dates and you may thus be able to gain some idea of my movements. We have taken part in every engagement which the second army have participated in since the very commencement of the campaign. We will now cheerfully struggle on until the end, which we hope is not too far off, especially if events continue as during the last eight days. The guns have not ceased a moment day or night during that time, while it has also rained incessantly and torrentially. We have been exposed to this without tents or cover or a change of clothes.

We left home shores on August 13th and arrived here on August 15th. It rained heavily and continued for twenty-four hours, and we marched through it to a supposed rest camp, but the 'rest' consisted in laying down in mud which was any depth to a foot. Sunday was fairly fine and we were able to dry up a bit. On Monday, at 2.30am, we entrained for a twenty-four hours' journey and this was our most enjoyable time up to date. At every small place on the route at which the train stopped, we were loaded with gifts and favours and our train was one mass of flowers and flags. The people, in fact, were frantic with enthusiasm. At many places, local bands regaled us with

'Le Marseillaise' and 'God Save the King', while the French people's attempt to imitate our cheers was an amusing 'Peep! Peep! Hoora!'

The letter continues with details of the war at the Front, its casualties, atrocities committed by the Germans and endless fatalities. However, he finishes his letter with, 'Believe me, I am in good health and the best of spirits.'

A photo of Belgian refugees who had recently arrived at Exeter. The photo was published in the Exeter and Plymouth Gazette of Wednesday 14 October 1914.

Exeter staff of the Young Men's Christian Association pictured in October 1914. When the men of the Devon Territorials moved from Woodbury to Perham Down, Salisbury Plain, the recreation tents, supplied by the YMCA, went with them.

A gathering of the Exeter Athletic Volunteer Corps. The picture appeared under the headline, 'For Home Defence' in the **Exeter and Plymouth Gazette** *of Thursday 15 October 1914.*

On Wednesday 14 October, the Mayor of Exeter welcomed a party of 100 Belgian refugees to the city. The party, which was the largest group to reach the city at one time, arrived at St David's Station at 6.30 and were greeted with cordiality and hospitality.

The week commencing 26 October saw the production *The Great Adventure* dramatised at the Theatre Royal.

A group of wounded soldiers, together with nurses, at the West of England Eye Infirmary in Exeter, which had been converted into a military hospital. The photo appeared in the **Western Times** *of Friday 16 October 1914.*

The Highland Light Infantry passing by the Guildhall on 21 October 1914. Members of the infantry played their bagpipes as they paraded down High Street. Young children, as well as adults, turned out to cheer them on and many young boys joined in the march.

Canadian troops at Fairfield, St Thomas. On Wednesday 21 October 1914, Canadian troops left Exeter and were cheered en route. Children of the Mint School were allowed out of their classes to watch them as they paraded along Fore Street.

Miss Eva Guildford-Quin, who appeared at the Theatre Royal during October 1914 in **The Great Adventure.** *The show had played over 650 times at the Kingsway Theatre in London. Miss Guildford-Quin was Australian by birth and had only recently come to Britain. Her charming personality was said to have secured her many friends amongst British theatre-goers.*

The *Western Times* of Thursday 29 October reported that the Canadian soldiers who had passed through Exeter from Plymouth the week before were delighted with the warmth and welcome they received, especially from the 'hospitable folk' in St Thomas. People in the vicinity of where the troops camped overnight made a great effort to make their short stay pleasant. A Mr Kerswell placed the Fair Field at their disposal and the authorities made arrangements for the troops to be billeted in the King's Hall. As soon as the men were settled, they enquired about restaurants, eager to supplement their army rations. Once people realised that the Canadians were roughing it, there was a host of invitations from local families who happily shared meals with the young soldiers. A sergeant-major of one of the contingents received enough offers of free billets from residents of Exeter to house all of the Canadians, and it was said that the men would have been a lot more comfortable had the military authorities allowed them to accept the kind offers. Fruit, food and cigarettes were given to the troops by locals and all were greatly appreciated.

On Friday 30 October 1914, the **Western Times** *published a photo of the Exeter University College Contingent of the 4th Devon Territorials on their way to India.*

On Tuesday 3 November, the *Exeter and Plymouth Gazette* reported on wounded troops in Exeter. The article said that of the 200 soldiers undergoing treatment at the VAD hospitals in Exeter, many had been discharged as convalescent. The remainder included more serious cases but all were said to be progressing favourably. Temporary Hospital No 3 (the Children's Home in Heavitree Road) had now been mobilised and more wounded were expected to soon be drafted to Exeter.

Lieutenant R. E. Hancock of Devon Regiment, whose deat reported in the **Exeter and Plymouth Gazette** *of 6 Nove 1914.*

On Monday 30 November, the *Western Times* announced that the first professional footballers to join the colours from the West of England were Exeter City players. These included Green and Cowie as well as the team's trainer Greenaway. It was noted that player Green was also an expert motorcyclist who had been anxious to enlist earlier. On Friday 27 September, he informed the chairman of the directors that he was to leave, and instantly volunteered for the 4th Devon Territorials for service in India. He was congratulated by the management for setting a fine example to other professional players.

Greenaway's departure was announced next and Green left for his home in the north of England to join his regiment there. The article mentioned that he had been in the army previous to the war but had bought himself out when he discovered he had a talent for football.

The paper stated:

It is highly satisfactory to learn that the example to single professionals, without domestic responsibilities, comes from the Exeter camp. Those who have severely criticised professional

Bombardier A. Ward, whose photo appeared in the **Exeter and Plymouth Gazette** *of Saturday 21 November 1914, was injured by shrapnel from a German shell, at Ypres. At the time of the article he was recovering in hospital at Thorpe Hill and had been inspected by the king. Bombardier Ward was the son of ex-Sergeant-Major Ward of 23 Elmside, Exeter.*

Com-Sergt.-Major Albert Sto Exeter, who died of wounds serving with the Devon Reg on 24 November 1914.

footballers and young followers of the game may say that the example is set rather late in the day, but certainly it is set better late

The Exeter RAMC men at the front as pictured in the **Western Times** *of Friday 27 November 1914. Many of the men featured in the photo were Exeter railway employees.*

than never, and one will not easily forget in the City Club's favour that their players were first in the field.

On Saturday 5 December, men wearing sandwich boards paraded through the main thoroughfares of Exeter displaying posters asking for 250 men to enlist after an appeal for men to join the Expeditionary Force, which was to be known as Exeter's Own. Mr E. Plumber, who organised the parade, also arranged for a display of the posters inside and

The **Coventry Evening Telegraph** *of Monday 30 November 1914 carried a picture of Corporal E. Radley, who was wounded at Ypres on 6 November and later died at a hospital in Exeter. He was aged 30 and left a wife and child.*

Exeter City football players in 1914. On Monday 30 November, the Western Times *announced that the first professional footballers to join the colours from the west of England were Exeter City players. These included Green and Cowie as well the team's trainer, Greenaway.*

The Exeter Cathedral School Cadet Corps off to Cullompton, on Wednesday 2 December 1914, to take part in a recruiting meeting.

Sergeant Norman Hill, from Exeter, of the 1st Coldstream Guards, whose death was reported in the Western Times *of Friday 4 December 1914. The article stated that Sergeant Hill had recently been killed at the Front. It was said that he had made splendid headway since joining the army and his career was full of promise. His mother, who lived in Exeter, heard the news of his death in a short note from a regimental friend. The letter concluded with the words, 'Do not grieve. We are all ready to die for our country and our honour.'*

On Saturday 5 December 1914, an advert appeared in the Exeter and Plymouth Gazette *stating 'Remember Belgium – Enlist Today'. The text below read:* Look at the above! Ask yourselves why you allow a team of hired footballers from the North – unfortunately described by the misnomer of Exeter City – to disport themselves in an arena in the centre of Exeter – the Ever Faithful – today to demonstrate to the citizens how easy it is to continue to play, provided you can deafen your ears to the moan of outraged girls and murdered babes, and to the appeal of those brave men who are dying for their country and calling for the aid which comes only too slowly. Among the spectators at St James's Park, this afternoon, will probably be many young fellows who have so far declined to discharge their duty to the land which gave them birth. To them we would say 'Be men! No longer show preference for the feather bed of the craven to the hero's death on the battlefield.'

outside Exeter City's football ground with the aim to get footballers to enlist. Special rosettes in the city's colours were issued to any man joining and were to be worn as a badge of honour.

On 11 December, approximately a thousand troops passing through Queen Street Station in Exeter, just after 7am, were given a 'parcel of refreshment' each, together with hot tea. The refreshments were distributed by the staff of Messrs Spiers and Pond on instruction of the mayoress. The money for refreshments came from the local hospitality fund. The morning was said to be 'stormy and cheerless', and it was reported that the refreshments and parcels were quite unexpected by the men, who were all pleased by the kindness.

The *Western Times* of Saturday 12 December stated that £300 was needed to provide entertainment for soldiers stationed at Exeter during Christmas. The residents of the city had already given very generously so far and it was hoped that the money could be raised in time. The newspaper reported the donations that had been submitted the day before. These included:

Private A. Roach, of the 1st Devons, who was from St Sidwell's, Exeter, was killed in action at Festubert on 30 October 1914. He left a widow and five children and had previously fought in the South African War. His picture appeared in the **Exeter and Plymouth Gazette** *of Friday 11 December 1914 under the headline 'Exeter Hero'.*

Mayoress of Exeter £5, Alderman T. C. Pring £5, Mr and Mrs Tozer 10s, Mrs and Miss Janson 5s, 'Sonny' 2s, Mr G. L. Boundy 10s, E.B. 5s, Three little schoolgirls 3s, Mrs Sanders £1 1s and Miss Tanner 1s.

The money deposited on Saturday 10 December, in the collecting box outside the Guildhall, amounted to 9s 6d.

A letter received from a Private James Kinaham of the Somerset Light Infantry, serving at the Front, was received at the mayoress's depot on Friday 11 December. It read:

On behalf of my comrades and myself, who comprised a draft of the S.L.I., I wish to return thanks to the Mayoress of Exeter and the Committee of Ladies for their kindness in presenting us with a very welcome parcel of refreshments each when we had a short stay in

*...er Alford of the 6th
...oons, who came from
...iton Fitzpaine and who
...killed in action on 20
...mber 1914. His picture
...ared in the newspaper of
...ay 11 December 1914.*

Exeter on route to our present station. This draft passed through on December 2nd and we were, all told, 225 men. I cannot find words to express the appreciation of ourselves at your kind consideration.

The *Western Times* of Monday 14 December reported on the formation of the Exeter's Own battalion:

Among the thousands of the sons of the Dominions beyond the Seas, who have answered the Empire's call, and are either at home training, or in England on route for the Front, are a number of Exonians and many Devonians. On Saturday, one young Colonial, Exeter born, took the King's shilling as a member of 'Exeter's Own' Company. He is Mr Horace Attwood of 75 Park Road.

Returning to the city a few days ago, Mr Attwood, who is 30 years of age, heard of the call which, on behalf of the King, the Mayor of Exeter is making for men to join an 'Exeter's Own' Company, and hearing, has answered, thus setting a splendid example to other Exonians and emulating that set by other members, who, earlier this week, were proud to have the civic badge pinned to their breasts.

The week in which the promoters wished to complete the 'Exeter's Own' Company reached its closing stages without the hopes being realised. In fact, as well might the appeal have been made to a stone wall as the hundreds of young men of the City, who have been shamed by the less than a dozen stalwarts, who proudly wear the 'Exeter's Own' colours. But the roll of honour at the Guildhall must be filled sooner or later and the sooner this is realised the better.

Now that the call for men for

A recruitment advert which appeared in the Exeter and Plymouth Gazette of Friday 11 December 1914. It calls for men to 'Fall in' and to 'Answer Now in Your Country's Hour of Need'.

India has been answered, perhaps that for 'Exeter's Own' will bear more fruit.

The week-end will give the truths that have been rammed home during the week by Press and by military official parades, time to sink into the hearts and minds of hangers-back and, perhaps, they will realise that such an opportunity is one that is unique

A selection of toys made by the girls of Exete had been thrown out of work during the wa toys were on view at the mayoress's depot nex to the Guildhall. The picture appeared in the **Plymouth Gazette** *of Tuesday 15 Dec 1914.*

A photo showing a family of Belg appeared in the **Western Times** *during December 1914 under the headline 'Safe from the Huns at Last'. The caption read: 'Anyone see that these poor people are hap and little wonder, for they are at safe from the Huns. They are Bel refugees, wives and daughters of fisher folk. The old lady is 82 yea age but the Germans have no resp for grey hairs. For weeks, they we beating about at the mercy of the storms in small fishing smacks, o being able to lie down in turns. N they are receiving every kindness the hands of the good Sisters at th Exeter Convent.'*

On Wednesday 16 December 1914, the Taunton Courier and Western Advertiser *announced that Sergeant-Major Hood had been given a commission as lieutenant and quartermaster in the 1st Reserve of the 5th Battalion Somerset Light Infantry.*

and must be taken. There is no consistency about the man who protests that he is prepared to take up arms but will wait until he is compelled.

The *Exeter and Plymouth Gazette* of Tuesday 15 December carried a photo of the late Sergeant G.T.

In the **Western Times** *during December 1914, this picture appeared under the headline 'Smokes for Devonshire Soldiers at the Front'. The caption read: 'The Devons and Devonshire Territorials at the Front are not to be forgotten at Christmas. The Mayoress of Exeter's Fund is to provide them each with either a pipe and tobacco or a large tin of cigarettes. Over 2,500 packages are now on their way, each containing a line of friendly and seasonable greeting. The picture shows the Mayoress (kneeling), helping to pack. Behind her the Mayor is standing. The pile of tins shown is only a small portion of the whole.'*

White, who was a member of the 1st Devons and was killed in action at Festubert on 30th October. He had formerly played for the Exeter FC Reserves and had been the captain of the Plymouth and District League team.

On Saturday 19 December, the *Western Times* announced that troops in Exeter would be allowed to use public houses in the area up until 9.30pm each evening as long as their good conduct continued. The decision came from the commander-in-chief of the Southern Command and was relayed to Colonel Western, the officer commanding No. T district.

An advert in the **Exeter and Plymouth Gazette** *of December 1914 encouraging men to enlist in the armed forces. It reads: 'Follow me! Your country needs you.' The newspaper was very patriotic and encouraged all young men to join the armed forces.*

Previously, although all premises were open until 9.30pm, soldiers had to leave half-an-hour earlier than civilians. It was felt that the good conduct of the troops didn't warrant them being treated differently from everyone else and the order was greeted with much gratitude.

On 22 December, a train carrying seventy wounded soldiers to

Private E. Bradford of the 2nd Devons who was killed in action and whose photo appeared in the **Exeter** *and* **Plymouth Gazette** *of Tuesday 22 December 1914. He was the son of Mr and Mrs Bradford of Ida Cottages, Paris Street, Exeter.*

Scout Patrol Leader William H. Newton, of Newton Poppleford, aged 13 years, who in five days collected £3 15s for the Mayoress of Exeter's Fund for cigarettes and tobacco for the gallant Devons at the Front. The photo appeared in the **Exeter** *and* **Plymouth Gazette** *of Thursday 24 December.*

Plymouth passed through Exeter where members of the Exeter Voluntary Aid Detachment waited for them. The soldiers were provided with refreshments and it was reported that 'there were very few serious cases'.

The *Western Times* of Saturday 26 December announced the opening of this year's pantomime, *Mother Goose*, at the Exeter Theatre.

Described as 'the children's Christmas treat', the newspaper noted that most of the players in the production were female with many of the male actors now enlisted in the army.

The paper noted that the pantomime had helped the drapery trade:

It creates a certain demand for the evening fabrics and trimmings on the drapers' shelves for which there has other wise been little call for this season. Exeter's Pantomime, 'Mother Goose', has, for instance, a wardrobe-mistress (Miss Glynn) and staff busy for weeks with silks and velvets and spangles in the wardrobe-room of Exeter

Exeter men serving on HMS Lion. The photo appeared in the Western Times of Thursday 24 December 1914 under the headline 'Exeter Jack Tars in the North Sea'.

Theatre where a gorgeous array of bright-hued costumes, that will offer on Boxing Day and for many days thereafter, a cheering contrast to the sombreness of present-day street attire, has been seen by one of our representatives.

The *Western Times* of Monday 28 December announced that the pantomime *Mother Goose* was a 'conspicuous success'. The article read:

Mother Goose made her appearance for the first time in Exeter on Boxing Day and how welcome the visit is likely to prove during the next few weeks may be measured by the bubbling mirth she provoked, the charm of the picture she presented to admiring eyes and the joyous enthusiasm that abounded during the matinee and evening performances which were witnessed by packed houses. This

The inside of the motor ambulance presented to the DVAO during December 1914

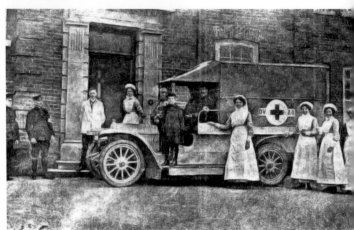

The motor ambulance presented to the DVAO outside No 3 Temporary Hospital as shown in the Exeter and Plymouth Gazette *of 24 December 1914.*

year's pantomime at the Theatre Royal promises, notwithstanding the war cloud that overhangs everything, to eclipse in popularity and successful production anything done in this way by the Theatre management for many a year.

On 30 December, the mayoress received a letter from a Lieutenant-Colonel R. Pickard, who was commanding the 24th Field Ambulance, 8th Division at the Front. The letter thanked the mayor and mayoress for Christmas gifts received. A letter was also received on behalf of officers, non-commissioned officers and men of the 4th Devon Regiment thanking the mayor and mayoress for tea and entertainment given to them on Christmas Day at Exeter.

The letter read:

The programme was much appreciated by those who were able to attend. Those who were unable to do so through duty are very grateful for the presents which have been sent to them since and heartily thank the Mayor and Mayoress for their kindly thought.

The mayoress put out an appeal for mufflers and mittens, which were said to be badly needed by the troops.

Kitchener's recruitment poster, 'Your country needs you!' A huge recruitment campaign encouraged young men to join up. By January 1915, almost one million men had enlisted. Pals battalions encouraged many to enlist and they ultimately provided enough men for three battalions.

CHAPTER TWO

1915 – Deepening Conflict

The *Exeter and Plymouth Gazette* of 1 January 1915 carried a story about the Christmas gifts that had arrived from America. It read:

> *All recognise the goodwill that prompted our American cousins to send a Santa Claus ship to Europe for the benefit of the little ones of the various nations, whose fathers are engaged in the war. But, unfortunately, when the cargo for England, unloaded at Plymouth by the Jason, was unpacked, it was quickly seen that there would be by no means sufficient presents for children in the United Kingdom whose fathers had been killed at the front or are at present fighting. Exeter's share of the cargo arrived in the city four days before Christmas and consisted of three cases. When these were unpacked, they were found but to contain a very limited number of toys, the rest, for the most part, being clothing, chiefly adult, some new but the majority second-hand. In addition, there were some packets of nuts etc.*

The *Western Times* of 2 January reported that an Exeter officer had appeared in the New Year's Honours List. The article read:

> *Congratulations to Flying Lieutenant Edward Osmond, son of Mr Edward Osmond, of Rewe near Exeter, and nephew of Mr Henry Osmond of Exeter, whose name appears in the New Year's Honours List on promotion to Flight Commander. His advance in the service has been very rapid. He was through the war from Mons until just*

Women employed by the City Collar Works. When the collar factory opened in 1912 it employe[d] between 400 and 500 women and girls. The factory had fifty iron machines and fifty hand irons. Th[e] work continued throughout most of the war but a strike was called in September 1918 over low pa[y]

recently when he was recalled to Gosport to organise a new flying squadron.

On Tuesday 5 January, the *Western Times* carried a story under the headline 'Exeter City Footballers with the Colours.' It read:

A letter has been received at the Express and Echo office from S. Greenaway, trainer to the Exeter City F.C., who is on his way to India with the second foreign service contingent of the 4th Batt. Devon Regt. T.F. He states that all the troops on board the ship he is crossing in have enjoyed excellent health since passing through the Bay of Biscay. 'We understand,' he says, 'that we have a duty to perform and we all mean to do our very best. It is no holiday; it is serious work in a serious time. Our voyage, so far, has been without incident and if people could only see our Navy's ships at sea, they would not be always asking, 'What is our Navy doing?'

Green, the Exeter City player, is on another troopship on his way to India.

F. Goddwin, Exeter City F.C., outside-left, has joined the

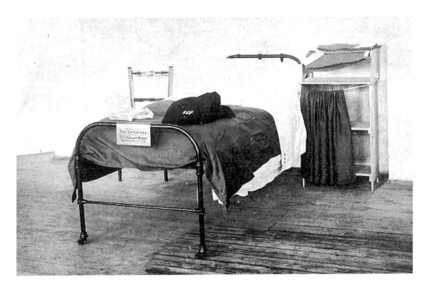

A VA Hospital bed sponsored by the employees of the City Collar Works. The total number of beds in Exeter military hospitals was 570 of which, during September 1915, 520 were occupied.

Footballers' Battalion and has proceeded to London for military duty.

On Tuesday 12 January, the *Exeter and Plymouth Gazette* published part of a letter received from Private Rabjohns, who was serving with the 24th Field Ambulance. It read:

We had a very useful lot of things from the Mayoress and some cigarettes for Christmas. We have this tea-time also received the cake which was so kindly sent. It was thoroughly enjoyed by all. How kind it is of the folks to do so much for us! Exeter has gained a great name for herself among the soldiers and no doubt the Mayoress and her party would be highly pleased to hear how the soldiers speak of those parcels of food and comforts, which were given out to them in the train when they landed at Plymouth and travelled through to Exeter. When they ask where we R.A.M.C come from, we tell them 'Exeter'. They say: 'Oh yes, we know Exeter. We passed through the station and were given fine parcels there.' Others say the packets of refreshments which the Mayoress's party gave them were worth half-

a-sovereign to them there, as they were so hungry and tired. We all value very much what Exeter is doing for us. It makes a great deal towards our happiness.

On Friday 29 January, Sir Robert Newman, the president of the Exeter Conservative Association, spoke at the St Thomas Constitutional Club. He said that with regard to carrying the war to a successful conclusion, conscription shouldn't be a consideration. He went on to say that, in his view, no war should be carried out against the wishes of the people. He also stated that no employer should put pressure on an employee to enlist in the colours.

On Sunday 31 January, with worries of a possible air-raid, Exeter decided to reduce the lighting in Exeter as a matter of precaution. Rumours circulated that the lights of an airship were visible in the south-western sky on Saturday evening causing much commotion. A large crowd, ignoring official instructions that they should find shelter, headed towards Martin's Lane and watched the lights for a considerable time. Many felt sure they saw it change position, head towards the city, and felt that a bomb would drop on the cathedral at any moment. After staring at the light for quite a while, many came to the conclusion that they were either just looking at a bright star or the lights of a British aircraft. The light eventually disappeared.

On Monday 1 February, the *Western Times* reported that a winner of the Victoria Cross from Exeter was to be received by the Mayor of Falmouth. The story read:

Bandsman Rendle, V.C., D.C.L.I., will today (Monday) be welcomed to Falmouth by the Mayor and Corporation. On Thursday last, he was received by the Mayor and Corporation of Launceston. Although belonging to the Duke of Cornwall's Light Infantry, Bandsmen Rendle is a Devonian and his home is at Exeter.

The *Western Times* of 9 February carried the story of a PC Townhill's experiences at the Front. It read:

Police Constable R. Townhill, a member of the Exeter City Force, has had some strange experiences at the Front. For five months, he escaped shells, bullets and bayonets, and was mentioned early in the war in dispatches, and then at last fell a victim, just before

Christmas, to a ladder accident, simple, but bad enough to result in him being out of action ever since.

When the war broke out, Townhill had been in the Exeter Police about five months. Before that, he had been stationed at Topsham Barracks with the R.F.A. He had joined the 33rd Battery at his home in Canterbury in 1911 and had been stationed at Woolwich and Bulford before coming on to Exeter. Having left the Army, of course, he was still a Reserve and thus, at the very start of the war, had to leave his police colleagues, with whom he had become a general favourite, and don his khaki as a bombardier of the 29th battery, the one to which he was drafted into the first Expeditionary Force. Last week, he was invalided home, and much to his surprise, and certainly to his keen gratification, he was brought to Exeter for hospital treatment. He is now at the Pennsylvania Temporary Hospital and it was at this institution that a Western Times representative found him on Saturday.

He is now rapidly mending from his accident, and a bad attack of influenza which followed it, and is, in fact, something like his old self again. He is still as quiet and modest, however, as he was as a member of the City Force, and the act of gallantry which earned for him mention in General French's despatches is the last thing one can get him to talk about. Anything else he will converse upon – all manner of ups and downs in fact but never that incident at the Battle of Mons. Exonians will remember the brief record that was made of it in these columns at the time and how, shortly afterwards, Townhill wrote us his own version because he feared he was getting overdue credit and wanted the simple facts known. On Saturday, he told our representative that what he wrote then was all he could possibly tell, adding, however, that the first he knew of having been mentioned in despatches was from the Express and Echo when a copy was sent out to him at the Front by his former Exeter colleague, PC Weeks.

On the evening of Tuesday 10 February, the mayor presided over a meeting of the City Council. One of the subjects discussed was what precautions Exeter should take if it were to come under a Zeppelin attack. A Mr Challice stated that gas and electric lights should be instantly turned off. However, it occurred to him that there may be a grave risk to life if gas was suddenly turned off at night and then turned

A Zeppelin preparing for flight. With the outbreak of war, Germany made great use of Zeppelins recognisance and bombing raids. In 1910, they were first flown commercially by Deutsche Luftschiffah AG (DELAG) and, by 1914, they had carried 34.000 pasengers on 1,500 separate flights.

on again where there were fires and gas jets burning in bedrooms. The mayor announced that there were arrangements being made to tackle the problems suggested by Mr Challice and that Exeter would be divided into sections so that officials could enter houses and make examinations before the gas was turned back on. It was said, however, that a raid was highly improbable.

On Monday 1 March, the *Western Times* carried a story about 'Exeter Athletes Volunteer Force'. It read:

The Right Worshipful, the Mayor of Exeter (Mr J G Owen) has consented to preside at a public meeting of citizens to be held at the Guildhall on Thursday evening next, when it is proposed to publicly inaugurate the City of Exeter Regiment, and start a fund for its equipment. The Exeter Force is affiliated to the Central Association Volunteer Training Corps, under which the members will be recognised as combatants in case of invasion and will be supplied with the War Office brassard in due course. The Mayor of Exeter has been appointed military commandant and Mr T Moulding, M.I.C.E., commandant. Citizens are invited to attend the meeting and support the movement. The Committee will be grateful to receive subscriptions to be announced at the meeting. A special parade of the Force has been announced for Thursday evening and they will attend accompanied by the band.

On 3 March, Privates Charles Godfrey and David Ray of C Company 4th Battalion Highland Light Infantry, Plymouth, appeared in court in Exeter charged with being absent from their regiment without leave since 1 March. Evidence was given by PC Skinner who stated that the defendants had asked him to show them the way back to the town barracks. In court, Inspector Sandford stated that an escort was being sent from Plymouth to take them back. They were remanded in custody and the PC received a reward of five shillings.

On Saturday 20 March, it was announced by the Elementary Education Sub-Committee that children would not be able to use the Exeter Swimming Baths for the season because they were currently being used by the troops. Arrangements were made, however, for a timetable to take effect as soon as the baths became available. It was hoped that a swimming gala would take place there in July.

On 25 March, the 3/4th, 3/5th and 3/6th Battalions of the Devonshire Regiment were formed at Exeter, Plymouth and Barnstaple before all being moved to Barnstable in August.

On Saturday 27 March, the official inspection of the local Volunteer Force took place at the county ground. Residents of Exeter were invited to attend. The force paraded at Bedford Circus at 3pm and were led by their band, in full uniform, to the county ground where they were inspected by Colonel Graeme who had been appointed by the Central Association Volunteer Training Corps. Their instructor, Colour-

On Wedneday 14 April 1915, a lady ticket-collector commenced duty at St David's Station, Exeter. She was a Miss Hopping who was the daughter of an Exeter railway official. She carried out the duties normally handled by male workers who were away fighting. The **Western Times** *commented: 'We congratulate Miss Hopping upon the distinction of being the first lady on platform service in Exeter. A woman who takes a man's place so that the man may go to the war is doing her little bit to help her country in a very real sense.'*

Sergeant Aplin of the 4th Devons, put the volunteers through their paces before a march-past. A request for more volunteers was issued and men over the age of 38 were invited to hand in their names on the day.

The *Lady's Pictorial* for the week ending 9 April included a section entitled 'Exeter's War Workers'. The full-page article featured numerous war activities carried out by women living in the city. One photo showed the mayoress with her helpers at her depot sorting out and packaging garments, etc, which had been contributed to help soldiers and sailors serving overseas. A section entitled 'Women and the Farm' showed female workers sheep-shearing, ploughing and leading farm horses. An article by Viscountess Wolseley was entitled 'The National Food Supply and Women's Vegetable Gardens'. In the article, she stated:

> *In Belgium, by means of intensive cultivation, a man is able to keep himself and family upon one acre and to become rich if he possesses two or three acres. Why are many more Englishmen and Englishwomen not getting one acre of land to yield, in one year, 32,400 head of lettuce and 16,200 head of celery which, according to the figures of the Liege Horticulture College, yielded together £130?*

On 16 April 1915, a photograph appeared of the actress Claire Romaine, under the headline 'Actresses Work for Soldiers at Exeter'. The article read: 'Miss Claire Romaine (on the left) ope. the sweetmeat week at Exeter. Th ladies of the Sweetie-Sweetie Chorus of the 'Sugar and Spice' Revue at Exeter Theatre Royal a this week selling sweetmeats at Exeter in aid of the Mayoress Fu and the Belgian Refugee Fund. They have a stall at the Devon a Somerset Stores, High Street, an are doing good business.'

The *Exeter and Plymouth Gazette* of Tuesday 4 May reported the many gifts that were donated to the Exeter VA Hospitals. As well as money there were also gifts of flowers, eggs, vegetables, salmon, jam, cakes, tobacco and cigarettes, books, butter, and magazines and newspapers. Other items included dominoes, tennis balls, feathers, slippers, towels, bandages, chairs, walking sticks and a musical instrument.

The number 5 hospital made an appeal for a bagatelle board, gramophone and piano for their recreation room.

Members of the Royal Engineers (Territorials) serving at Gibraltar pictured in May 1915. They were formally employed at Messrs Willey and Co's works at Exeter.

On Wednesday 19 May, 200 wounded soldiers, who were being cared for in Exeter's military hospitals, were taken on a motor drive to Sidmouth. The trip was the idea of Dr Bingley Pullen but, at first, there was great difficulty finding enough cars to organise the trip. The Exeter Automobile Association took over the organisation and an appeal to their members saw the loan of sixty cars (all from Mr W. A. Dagsworthy of the Sidmouth Garage), which were not only sufficient to carry the wounded soldiers but also able to take some nurses and orderlies who were needed to look after the soldiers.

Many people watched the gathering of cars and the troops as they met up at the Gordon Lamp at Heavitree before continuing their journey to Sidmouth.

The convoy arrived at their destination at two o'clock and the town was decorated with flags and bunting in honour of the visit. Crowds of people lined the streets to meet them and watched as the long fleet of cars proceeded along the Esplanade.

The troops were entertained at the Manor Hall and Dr Bingley Pullen and his three daughters arranged entertainment and made sure that their visit was as pleasant as possible.

The programme opened with Miss Gladys Ainsworth playing a piano solo. The Reverend W. S. Airy contributed two popular songs, and dances by Mrs W. Crees and Miss J. Pullen (both daughters of Dr Pullen) gave great pleasure. Mrs Crees also sang *Moon-struck* before singing a duo with her sister.

After the entertainment, tea was provided. Local theatre managers arranged for acts to entertain the troops but due to the length of the programme already provided, there was no time left for them to appear.

On Monday 24 May, the 2nd/1st Cyclist Company South Midland Mounted Division paid a visit to Exeter during a training march. The company consisted of 200 men and was under the command of Captain Langdon Thomas. The cyclists commenced their journey on Sunday morning at Gloucester before travelling down to Bristol. They carried on to Bridgwater before arriving in Exeter at 1.15pm. One man was thrown from his bicycle near Wellington and sustained bruises and scratches. The Boy Scouts met the company at both Bridgwater and Exeter and showed the cyclists to their respective billets. The cyclists

A photo of Exeter lads in India appeared in the **Western Times** *of Friday 28 May 1915. The caption read: 'A group of 4th Territorials at Wellington, India, including lads who won prominence in athletic circles of Exeter. Top row: H L Hall (Exeter), J Fenwick (Exeter), A Gibbings (Pinhoe). Second row: J Hobbs (Exeter), G Fenwick (Exeter), J M Tonkin (Truro). Bottom row: J Gaitch (Lyme Regis), F Newcombe (Exeter).'*

were found quarters in private houses and were very grateful for the generous way they were treated.

The Gloucesters left Exeter on Tuesday 25 May after parading at the 7th Devon Drill Hall in Longbrook Street at ten o'clock. They expected to reach Bridgwater between three and four o'clock and intended to stay the night before continuing on to Bristol.

On the evening of Friday 4 June, the band of the City of Exeter Regiment, the Athletes' Volunteer Force, gave their first concert as

The South Midland Cyclists at Exeter on Monday 24 May 1915. Some 200 men of the 2nd 1st Cyclist Company, South Midland Division, visited Exeter in the course of a training tour and were billeted in the city for the night. They left the following morning at ten o'clock for Bridgwater.

public entertainers on Northernhay under the command of Lieutenant F. S. Shobbrook. The money collected was contributed to the Mayoress of Exeter's war fund. The music played was described as 'of a light nature' and included Anciffe's *Nights of Gladness*, *The Chimes* and selections from *The Girl in the Taxi*. The

A section of the 2nd-7th (Cycle) Battalion Regiment in North Devon, while looking for recruits, in May 1915.

band's honorary secretary, Mr Charles Snow, announced that they would play again the following Friday.

The *Exeter and Plymouth Gazette* of Tuesday 8 June reported on the Whit-Monday military sports held by the Exeter Cycling Club. The event, which entertained wounded soldiers, made a profit of £29 1s 3d, which was forwarded to the Mayoress of Exeter to help one of her many funds. Mr F. W. Wood, the honorary secretary, wrote saying:

My Committee desire me to say that the wounded soldiers on the stand were entertained to tea and refreshments as well as cigarettes and, after doing this, we think the cheque we are able to send you is for a good amount. The Committee feel proud that they have been able to help your funds.

The 7th Devonshire Regiment with their bicycles.

On 11 June, Princess Victor Napoleon, more commonly known as Princess Clementine, opened a grand bazaar at the Palace Grounds, Exeter. Princess Clementine was the wife of Prince Victor Bonaparte and the daughter of King Leopold of Belgium. The event was held to raise funds for a convalescent home for wounded Belgian soldiers. The event was said to be one of the most important of its kind held in Exeter and was arranged quickly within the course of a week. It was explained that England and France had numerous convalescent homes for their troops in the South of France but Belgium had none. Many wounded Belgian soldiers had been nursed back to health in hospitals and convalescent homes in Devon but, it was felt, that all available places would soon be needed by British troops.

During the day Belgian badges were sold in the streets of Exeter by female Belgian refugees now living in the city. The flags of the allies were readily purchased and much admired while the Belgian flag flew on the Guildhall in preparation of Princess Clementine's visit.

The *Western Times* of Thursday 24 June reported the death of an Exeter soldier. The story read:

> *News has been received that Private Albert Perriam, of the 1st Devons, has been killed in action. He was well known in Exeter and only returned to the Front a fortnight ago, after having been wounded. He was 27 years of age and had seen service in Burmah, Crete, India and Egypt. His brother, Mr J Perriam, of 46 Cowick Street, Exeter, received a letter from deceased yesterday, while later in the day came a wire announcing his death.*

The *Western Times* of Friday 16 July reported on the inquest of an Exeter soldier who had died at Torquay from anthrax. Private Edwin G. Chenneour, aged 19, had previously served on the east coast and then moved to Devonport before moving to Paignton. His father stated that a small pimple had appeared on his son's face and, although painless, he was later admitted to Rockwood Red Cross Hospital at Torquay. Dr F. Crowdy stated that by the time he saw him, the pimple was a large boil, which was removed. The patient later complained of head pain and became unconscious during the night before dying on the Sunday morning. Dr Crowdy stated that he had no doubt that the death was caused by anthrax. It was thought that the disease was carried

Nurses of the Voluntary Aid Hospital No 1 in Exeter in July 1915. VA 1 occupied the West of England Hospital.

by a fly that had come into contact with an affected animal and was an isolated case. Doctors tried to get an anti-serum from France and Italy but none could be obtained. The jury returned a verdict of death by anthrax, although there was nothing to show how the disease had been contracted.

On Thursday 22 July, the *Western Times* featured a story about the 3rd Devons' appreciation of their treatment at Exeter. It read:

The 3rd Devons, who were recently quartered at Exeter, have sent £10 to the Mayoress of Exeter's Hospitality Fund, and Major Arundel, in forwarding the sum, pays a striking tribute to the many kindnesses which the Mayoress's Depot did for his men. He writes: 'I have much pleasure in sending you a cheque for £10 towards your deficit from the 3rd Devon

A postcard to a sweetheart showing a soldier kissing his loved one.

Regiment, with our most grateful thanks for all you have done for us. We trust your good cause will always prosper and flourish and never lack for plenty of supporters in such a good cause. The regiment have always appreciated your work, and still do. They can never thank you enough, in fact, for all you have done for them. You were always ready to help and never turned anyone away empty handed. We were all sorry to leave Exeter and shall always cherish grateful recollections of your many kindnesses.

On 11 August, a Mr Crawley, a leading London eye specialist, said that he had seen thirty-eight cases of war-eye while giving examinations at the Victoria Hall in Exeter. He stated that the amount of war workers in Exeter, who, because of intense concentration and eye straining whilst carrying out procedures such as needlework, etc, was leading to the new condition. He stated:

The Mayoress of Exeter supplying refreshments to troops during train stops. The food and tea was much appreciated by the men and many later wrote letters of thanks.

There is nothing serious about these cases, provided they are attended to in time. Many of them merely require a rest cure and general care and attention. The danger lies in neglect. The least suggestion of tiredness in the eyes, the least hint of headache or mental fatigue, should be sufficient warning.

Advice should be taken at once. To imagine that your eyes will get better of their own accord, or to rush off and buy a pair of spectacles that seem to suit, is the height of folly. I am making quite a speciality of War-eye cases and naturally extend my particular sympathy to such patriotic workers.

The *Exeter and Plymouth Gazette* advised that anyone who had the least suggestion of eye trouble should go and see him while he was in Exeter. His services were offered free between the hours of 10am to 1pm and 2pm to 7pm.

Members of the 2nd-4th Wessex Brigade, RFA (all Exeter boys) at Bangalore. The photo appeared Exeter and Plymouth Gazette of Friday 13 August 1915.

On Monday 16 August, the wedding took place of Private Albert Henry Cudmore, of the 1st Devonshire Regiment, and Miss Gertrude Isabella Passmore, both of Cyprus Terrace, Wonford. The bridegroom had been at the Front since the previous August and was back home on short leave before returning on Thursday 19 August. The bridegroom's brother, Private George Cudmore, was best man and the bride carried a bouquet tied with the Devons' colours. There was much interest in the wedding and friends and family formed a guard of honour as the couple left the church.

The *Western Times* of Monday 23 August reported on the hospitality that the troops had received from the mayoress and her helpers. The article read:

The Mayoress of Exeter's Hospitality Fund has many generous friends who spare no effort and make considerable sacrifices to provide the means of carrying on the service. Canon and Mrs Langford of Southbrook, Starcross, have been consistent supporters of the Mayoress's Depot from the beginning. On Thursday, they arranged a special sale of work at Southbrook for the Hospitality

Fund. Of course, they had the enthusiastic assistance of the leading residents of Starcross. The band of the Western Counties Institution gave their services, a much appreciated help. Canon and Mrs Langford gave the tea and Miss Gater of South Street, Exeter lent the china free of charge. In fact, everybody put his or her shoulder to the wheel. The result was that no less than £40 was realised and a cheque for that amount has been sent to the Mayoress of Exeter.

On Saturday, Starcross had its Forget-Me-Not Day so that altogether the town can fairly claim that it is doing its bit. The drain on the Hospitality Fund continues unabated so that the utmost effort is needed to keep the Fund in credit. The Mayoress and her ladies would hate to abandon the Hospitality part of their work which is of such practical utility. Some have said that the War Office ought to make better provision for feeding troops on route. That may be, but if the War office doesn't make arrangements, and heaven knows the War Office has so much in hand that some details may be overlooked, we must do what we can to repair the omission. The testimony of many Commanding Officers is on record that but for the hospitality shown at Exeter, the troops would be ten and twelve hours between meal and meal. Apart altogether from the mere question of hunger, there is the moving fact that the expression of kindness, this 'mothering' at the Exeter Station, touches the men.

The Territorial Force, APC Section, at St Sidwells, Exeter in 1915.

Their gratitude is pathetic. They are made to think that we are thinking of them, proud of them, as they leave our shores for the great adventure.'

On Tuesday 31 August, a soldier, Private Albert Edward Smart of the Suffolk Regiment, appeared before the Exeter police court. He was accused of obtaining under false pretences a pair of riding breeches and a pair of brown leggings, to the value of 24 shillings, from Joshua Daw. The accused had gone to Daw's shop one evening, stating that his employer, a Mr Biffen, had ordered the goods and would later pay for them. The accused took the items and no payment was forthcoming. The goods were later pawned.

The accused informed the court that since the offence, he had joined the army and hoped to fight for king and country. He also stated that he had got one other man to enlist in the army also.

The chief constable informed the court that the accused had appeared in court twenty times previously for various offences and had been in prison several times.

The king and queen visiting wounded soldiers in 1915. On Wednesday 8 September, the king and queen visited Nos 1 and 5 Military Hospitals, inspecting the buildings and conversing with practically every wounded man in the wards. In the grounds they met wounded soldiers from other hospitals in Devon. The king expressed the pleasure it gave him to see them and his pride at the manner in which they had fought.

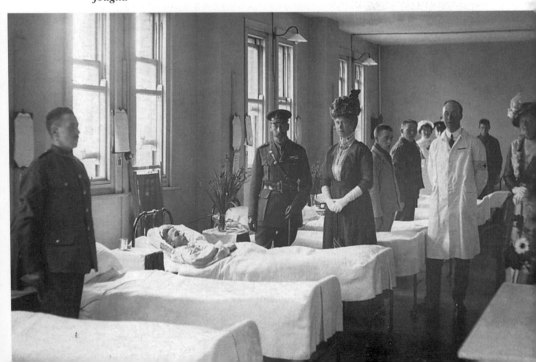

The king and queen visiting Exeter, welcomed by cheering crowds, during September 1915.

Queen Mary, accompanied by Dr Henry Davey, visiting VA Hospital No 5 in 1915. The walking wounded, nurses and staff turned out to greet her.

The court found the accused guilty and sentenced him to two months in prison with hard labour.

On 9 September, King George V and Queen Mary travelled back to Plymouth, arriving at North Road Station. They continued their visits to local hospitals and afterwards visited Devonport Dockyard, where they again awarded medals. In the evening, they once more travelled to Horrabridge before continuing their journey onwards to Exeter, where they paid a surprise visit.

The king and queen as they're driven through the streets of Exeter on Wednesday 8 September 1915. The king can be seen saluting the crowds.

On Tuesday 21 September, the *Western Morning News* reported on letters received from troops offering their grateful thanks for the hospitality given to them at Exeter. It read:

Captain W Brock of Exeter, writing from Alexandria, where he is recovering from his injuries, sends an inspiring note to the Mayoress of Exeter's Depot. It is one which we need not apologise for quoting in full.

'Just a line,' he says 'in time to catch this mail to inform you that Private W Lee of the Fusiliers, killed in action at Gallipoli Peninsula, had a 'Mayoress of Exeter' card in his pay book, which, with the contents of his pockets, came to us to be forwarded. I thought you would like to know that your memory was carried even unto death. Many of the men out here have your cards. You are making the name of Exeter to be a sweet-smelling savour in the nostrils of the British Army.'

What higher tribute can be paid but that?

This is the letter of a soldier's mother living at Woodford in Essex:

'My son was on the 'Empress of Britain' which stopped at Exeter some two or three weeks ago. The following is an extract from a letter we have received from him: 'At Exeter, we were presented with

a paper bag which contained a delicious ham roll, a piece of cake, and an apple or orange, also a packet of cigarettes, all the gifts of the Mayoress of the City. We wrote her a sort of round-robin in our carriage, which I sketched on, and then we all signed it.' In case that letter of thanks has not reached you after all, I am writing to show you how much your kindness was appreciated, and also to thank you from my husband and myself for your kindness to my son amongst others.'

Here is another brief note: 'The men and my fellow NCOs of the above draft have requested me as senior NCO to write and ask you to accept, on behalf of yourself and your Committee, our hearty thanks for the refreshments provided for us at Exeter. Further, I should like to add the cheery and pleasant way in which your helpers treated us was most delightful and refreshing to us all.'

A corporal of the Borderers, who received Hospitality Fund fare two months ago, writes:

'Your gift, I can assure you, was highly appreciated by us because in our hard life we get very little of the cake and sweets etc. The card, which was enclosed, I am keeping as a memento of the occasion. I would have written sooner thanking you but somehow I could not bring my mind to think that you would care to hear about it. Several of my comrades, however, have asked me to write at various times, and I now take the opportunity.'

There were several other messages in similar vein in yesterday's bulky letter bag.

The *Exeter and Plymouth Gazette* of Wednesday 29 September listed the amount of money that had been collected for both the hospitality and prisoners-of-war. The article also carried a request for a football from the 2nd/7th Devons who were on coast defence work in 'an isolated part of England'.

The *Western Times* of Monday 11 October reported the death of an Exeter soldier. The story read:

Sergeant Frank Barnes of the Wilts Regiment, whose death was reported in the Western Times of Monday 11 October 1915. He was the son of QMS Barnes, who was employed at the Infantry Record Office in Exeter.

QMS Barnes of 10 Albion Place, Exeter and now of the Infantry Record Office, Exeter, has received unofficial news of the death of his son, Sergeant Frank Barnes of the Wilts Regiment. The young man was well-known and much respected in Exeter where, before he joined the army, he was employed at the Devon and Somerset Stores. He was only 22 years of age and he had been in the service for four years. He was killed on September 25th, being shot in the head when storming a German first line trench. Sergeant Barnes has served at the Front throughout the war. He was wounded at Mons and came home but he returned to the fighting line in December and

On Friday 12 November 1915, two of the German guns captured by the 8th and 9th Battalions of Devonshire Regiment were brought to Exeter and handed over by the military authorities to the lo lieutenant of the county. They were subsequently drawn through the city and lodged at Northernhay. T photos show (1) one of the guns; (2) the handing-over ceremony at Queen Street Station; (3) Colonel Wal commanding No 8 District, calling for cheers for the Devons; (4) the Lord-Lieutenant chatting to some the heroes of Loos.

has been there ever since. General sympathy will be extended to Mr Barnes who has also had a brother killed in action.

The *Western Times* of 23 October reported that Exeter's effort for the British Red Cross Society had broken the City's records. Forty thousand Red Cross flags had been ordered by Exeter's Alexandra Day Committee, but these proved insufficient. On previous flag days, including Rose Day, the committee had always ordered a supply equal

German guns at Exeter, which were captured by the 8th and 9th Devonshire Regiment at Loos. The guns were later displayed at Northernhay Park.

to half of Exeter's population, with an additional two thousand. However, all forty thousand flags were sold and Exeter was reported as playing a highly credible part in the national Red Cross effort.

On Friday 12 November, there was great excitement at Exeter when two German guns captured by the 8th (Buller's Own) and 9th Devons at Loos were handed over to the county of Devon from the War Office.

A Red Cross VAD nurse. VAD nurses played a vital part in the First World War caring for injured soldiers who returned home from the Front.

Earl Fortescue requested that the Mayor of Exeter keep the guns in safe custody. He stated that after the bombardment of the German trenches on 25 September, the 8th Devons and the Gordon Highlanders led the attack. They came under heavy fire but reached the German first line. Many British officers were killed or wounded. The remaining officers split the men into two parties and charged the German line, capturing the whole German battery.

On Thursday 18 November, the *Western Times* carried a story under the headline, 'The Sheriff of Exeter's Joke Against Himself'. It read:

A neat story was told by the Sheriff of Exeter against himself at the opening of the St Thomas's Church sale of work yesterday. It related to an incident at the overflow meeting last Friday with connection to the recruitment scheme. Mr Stocker presided at the overflow meeting and it was his first public function since his election to the office of Sheriff. Mr Bowerman, MP, who addressed the meeting, in making some allusions to the rush of young men into matrimony in the hope, as they imagined, of escaping the early class of recruits under Lord Derby's scheme, when turning to the Sheriff, innocent of Mr Stocker's bachelorhood, remarked: 'I have the greatest possible contempt, Mr Sheriff, for a man who is a bachelor but –' The roar of laughter effectually cut off the rest of what Mr Bowerman intended to say. 'I enjoyed the fun as much as anybody,' was the Sheriff's comment, 'but for once, I confess, I did blush.'

The *Exeter and Plymouth Gazette* of Saturday 23 November covered a tale of theft at the No 1 VAD Hospital at Exeter. It read:

A remarkable story was related to the Exeter Magistrates yesterday when James Clay, 40, wardmaster at No 1 V.A.D. Hospital, Exeter, was charged with stealing £100 belonging to J.E. Payne. Mr Martin Alford appeared for the defendant.

The Chief-Constable said that on Saturday, November 9th, defendant was handed a cheque for £100 to cash. He cashed it on Monday, November 11th, but did not hand over the money. Next morning, he left the hospital and wasn't seen again until arrested at Nottingham with the money intact.

Defendant from the dock declared that he did not intend to steal the money or appropriate it to his own use. It was his duty to pay with the money the 3s 6d per week allowed to each man for pocket money. He had heard that his wife was ill and that a brother, whom he had not seen for ten years, was coming home on leave, so he went to his parents where he could easily be traced. He took the money for safety.

Further evidence showed the defendant, who had served in the South African campaign and the present war, had only been wardmaster for three weeks. It was stated that he had never provided a home for his wife nor had he supported her.

The Chairman (Mr H B Varwell) said that the defendant would be sentenced to three months in the second division. They made the latter condition in order to save his pension.

On Saturday 18 December, the *Exeter and Plymouth Gazette* carried an article about the city's forthcoming pantomime. It read:

Christmas is now drawing very near and the thoughts of the 'kiddies' are turned towards Father Christmas and, of course, the annual trip to the pantomime. True, it is war time and England is engaged in a stern conflict but even our gallant lads at the front or on the seas would not wish the youngsters should be denied their usual Christmas treat in the shape of a pantomime. Then, again, we have many lads in khaki or navy blue, either in training or on leave who will, doubtless, be glad of a night at the pantomime. Under all the circumstances, we are sure that the majority of proper thinking people will agree that Mr Percy Dunsford, the genial resident manager of the Theatre Royal, Exeter, has done the right thing in deciding to have 'business as usual' for the pantomime season this year.

The article went on to announce that this year's pantomime would be the ever popular *Babes in the Wood*.

CHAPTER THREE

1916 – The Realization

Compulsory enlistment for men between the ages of 18 and 41 was introduced for single men and childless widowers. However, essential war workers, clergymen, the physically unfit and approved conscientious objectors were exempt. The upper age was later raised to 51.

On Monday 3 January, the mayor appealed in the *Western Times* for Furber Ambulances. His letter read:

Sir, A few months ago, through the generosity of the public, I was able to send two Furber hand ambulances to each of our Devon battalions at the Front. The Commanding Officers were very glad to receive them and when I was visiting the Devons in France a fortnight ago, I received personally the thanks of officers and men who had tested the ambulances on actual service and proved their worth. The stretcher bearers were very proud to show them to me. The one complaint was that they would like four – one for each company – instead of two per battalion. The directors of the Western Morning News have kindly undertaken to present a third ambulance to each battalion so that there is only the fourth for each battalion to be found.

I am happy to say that the Exeter Municipal Officers, who gave two of the original ten sent out, have offered me two more, so that I only need three to ensure that each company of our five Devon battalions shall have a Furber ambulance for its very own.

I need not enlarge upon the advantages of this particular ambulance. The men at the front say that it is far and away the best, because not only is it more easily handled than any other type, but the pneumatic tyres enable our wounded to be removed from the firing line with a minimum of jolting and discomfort generally. I need approximately £54 to buy, pack, insure and defray carriage on those three ambulances. Anyone sending £18 will be the donor of an ambulance which will bear a metal plate recording the fact. But I shall be happy, of course, to receive any subscriptions, large or small, for this excellent purpose. Please endorse envelope 'Furber Ambulance.'

Yours truly, James G. Owen. Mayor. Guildhall, Exeter, January 3, 1916.

On Wednesday 9 February, wounded soldiers from various hospitals around and outside the city enjoyed high tea and entertainment in the Victoria Hall arranged by Mr E. S. Plummer. Approximately 400 men attended and came from hospitals in Exeter, Honiton, Crediton, Bystock, Exmouth, Topsham and Tiverton. They were conveyed to and from the Victoria Hall in motor cars provided by members of the Automobile Association. The City Corporation also lent two trams to take the men to the venue. The building was decorated with flags and bunting by Mr W. E. Hoyles and helpers. A platform had been set up at one end of the hall for performers and this was decorated with palm trees and ferns, which were supplied by Mr G. Kerswell of Bowhay Nurseries. Mr Plummer was unable to greet the guests due to the death of his brother. During the afternoon, a telegram was dispatched to him from the troops thanking him for his kindness and sympathising for his loss.

The tea included roast beef, mutton, boiled beef, ham and various sweets. Cigarettes, chocolates and bonbons were also distributed. Each table came under the charge of several ladies, who were assisted by male stewards and willing helpers.

The programme was arranged by Colonel Richards. Many performances were given by a troupe calling themselves 'The Smart Set' and included concert numbers as well as solo performances. They received much applause from the troops.

Other songs were performed by many local artistes and dances were performed by the pupils of Miss Rosa Couldridge. The Salvation Army also played various selections of music. Animated pictures were shown during the intervals and the event ended with the singing of the National Anthem.

On Saturday 11 February, upwards of 300 wounded men from various hospitals around the city were entertained at the Hippodrome by Mr and Mrs H. G. Morgan. All the professional artistes engaged at the Hippodrome for the week gave their services free. Some men attending were stretcher cases and were accommodated in the front stalls. During the interval, cigarettes were handed out to the men.

On Tuesday 15 February, it was announced that Exeter's lights would be further reduced due to the fear of Zeppelin raids. At a meeting of Exeter City Council, the mayor, Mr James G Owen, stated that there was now a good chance that Zeppelins may come further west and he felt that steps were needed to protect Exeter. After a meeting with the chairman of the Lighting Committee, it was decided that there would have to be a drastic reduction of the lighting in the city immediately. People with houses on a height were requested to cover up their night-time lighting. The *Western Times* of 16 February reported:

Mr Stocker, of the council, said that his Worship's statement would be read with considerable interest by the citizens. Up to now, they had been living under normal conditions, hardly aware that we were engaged in the deadly throes of war. The time has come when we must realise we are at war. New means would have to be provided to ensure public safety. Drivers of motors and other vehicles would have to realise that what has been a safe speed under existing conditions would be unsafe under conditions which would exist in a few days. They would have to go slower. Pedestrians too would have to realise that they must not walk in the roadways. Parents must be made to understand that children must not be in the streets after dark under the new conditions. Accidents were bound to occur and he hoped that if they happened to children, the fault would be put on the parents who allowed them to be in the streets. Certain neighbourhoods were particularly dangerous. It was necessary that darkness prevail along the Quay and the Canal Banks, notwithstanding that some sentimental jury might say that the fault was that the lights had been put out. He hoped that under the new

The Tercentenary of William Shakespeare's death was celebrated in 1916 and the photo shows part of celebrations held at Exeter.

conditions that no horned beasts would be driven through the streets after dark.

On Friday 12 May, the *Western Times* published a list of daily duties sent to them by an Exeter soldier. Under the headline 'Tommy's Daily Toll', this included:

6.30am Reveille – 'Christians Awake'.
6.45am Rouse Parade – 'Art thou weary, art thou languid?'
7am Breakfast – 'Meekly wait and murmur not.'
8.15am Company Parade – 'When He cometh.'
8.45am Manoeuvres – 'Fight the good fight.'
11.45am Swedish Drill – 'Here we suffer grief and pain.'
1pm Dinner – 'Come ye thankful people, come.'
2.15pm Rifle Drill – 'Go labour on.'
3.15pm Lecture by Officers – 'Tell me the old, old story.'
4.30pm Dismiss – 'Praise God from who all blessing flow.'
5pm Tea – 'What means this eager, anxious throng?'
6pm Free for the night – 'On lord, how happy we shall be.'
6.30pm Out of bounds – 'We may not know, we cannot tell.'
7pm Route March – 'Onward Christian Soldiers.'
10pm Last Post – 'All is safely gathered in.'
10.15pm Lights Out – 'Peace, perfect peace.'
10.30pm Inspection of Guards – 'Sleep on, beloved.'
11pm Night Manoeuvres – 'The day Thou gavest, Lord, is ended.'

On Wednesday afternoon of 31 May, wounded troops from No 1 and No 2 VAD hospitals in Exeter were entertained by the scholars of St James' Girls School. The headmistress, Miss Bamforth, had previously sent out invitations to the hospitals and large numbers of patients attended. The programme opened with the *Empire Pageant* showing Britannia, complete with Union Jack, together with performers appearing as Britain and the various countries making up her allies. Each had speaking parts and were met with much applause from the soldiers. There were then country dances followed by songs and a drill with red, white and blue flags. The performance was finished off with *Rule Britannia* before cigarettes were handed out to the troops.

On 1 April, the *Western Times* published a letter from 2nd Lieutenant AJF Chambers of the Warwickshire Yeomanry to the Mayoress of Exeter. It read:

A line to thank you on behalf of myself and my men for the refreshment you provided for us on Sunday night last, when we were travelling. You have no idea how much the hot tea and buns were appreciated. It was a very cold night and something hot was just what we wanted. With the warmest thanks to you and your committee.

Another letter from an officer commanding the Devon Regiment

A photo appeared in the **Exeter and Plymouth Gazette** *of Tuesday 2 May 1916 under the headline 'Exeter Boys Abroad'. The text below read: 'Exonians in the Devon Company, Royal Engineers. Their names are (reading from left to right): Sergt Hancock, Sappers F Camden, E Chatworthy and A Coles and Second-Corpl. James.'*

acknowledged a bale of 170 socks. He wrote: 'They will be very acceptable to all ranks in the Battalion.'

On Thursday 18 May, arrangements were made for a ceremony to be held at No 1 VAO Hospital in Magdalen Street. Two soldiers who fought at battles on the Western Front were to be decorated with the DCM. They were ex-Lance Corporal W. H. Tremlett of the Devon Regiment from Withycombe, Exmouth, and Sergeant D'Arcy of 1st Royal Irish Rifles who hailed from Dublin.

Ex-Lance Corporal Tremlett was awarded the DCM for gallantry at a battle at which the Germans used asphyxiating gas, which caused many casualties amongst the troops. Tremlett, together with a companion, left a trench to go out in heavy fire to rescue a man who had been overcome by fumes.

Sergeant D'Arcy was awarded the DCM for coolness displayed on the battlefield while controlling a gun under heavy fire. He had previously been noted for his good work on many occasions.

On Saturday 27 May, the Exeter Tribunal resumed it sittings presiding over cases appealing for exemption. The mayor, Mr J. G. Owen, oversaw events.

One case involved an application by a Mr Trick, who was the clerk of the St Thomas Union. He appealed for the exemption of Mr F. T. Moore, age 34, who was a workhouse master and deputy superintendent and registrar. An absolute exemption was asked for. It was stated that the staff of the St Thomas Workhouse had been greatly depleted.

A photo of 'a group of Exeter lads with the British Fleet' appeared in the **Exeter and Plymouth Gazette** *of Friday 12 May 1916.*

*Mayor: 'It looks as if it goes on much longer, you will have to come
to Exeter Workhouse!'*
  Mr Trick: 'I have no doubt that you will help us if necessary.'

Mr Moore was exempted until 30 November.

On 3 June, the *Western Times* reported on the heavy losses during
the naval battle at Jutland. The article reported:

*News of the great naval battle came through to Exeter at about 8pm.
The announcement, first received in this office over the telephone,
was quickly published by a special edition and otherwise and the
tidings rapidly spread throughout the city.*

  *Naturally, the news of this, the greatest naval engagement of the
war so far created a stir and not less so because the first impression
led many to conclude that the result was more unfavourable to us
than a reading of the detailed reports proved it to be.*

  *Large numbers quickly made their way to the offices of the
Western Times and Express and Echo and snapped up the special
edition as it was run off, hot from the press. From all parts of the
city too, and from various parts of the county, came urgent telephone
enquiries with the object of verifying the rumour of a big sea fight
and ascertaining such details that might be available, especially as
to the names of the ships sunk.*

  *Naturally, regret was freely expressed at the loss of so many
gallant lives and ships but there was nothing in the nature of a panic.
Frequently the opinion was to be heard that the British squadron
had, by some means, been caught at a disadvantage by superior
forces and further details on the manner and outcome of the fight
will be eagerly awaited.*

  *Similar scenes were to be witnessed in other Devon towns, where
the special messages sent out from this office were the first
intimation received of the event.*

On 15 June, the *Exeter and Plymouth Gazette* announced the
commencement of enrolment in the Volunteer Force in Exeter.
Magistrates present were Mr W Kendall King, an ex-mayor of Exeter,
Mr James Stokes and Mr Joseph Gould. Altogether, 101 men took the
oath of allegiance to the king and swore to 'faithfully serve His Majesty
in Great Britain for the defence of the same against his enemies and

oppressors whatsoever'. Volunteers upwards of ninety men had already been transferred to the reserves. The *Exeter and Plymouth Gazette* went on to report:

> *Exeter is assured of a Company but this certainly should not be considered sufficient. In a city with a population of 60,000, surely two Companies, the full strength of which is 500 men, should be forthcoming. The old objection that some people had that the volunteers had no status, has now, of course, disappeared and it is the duty of every able-bodied man, who has a few hours of leisure at his disposal each week – and practically everybody is in that position – to stand boldly forward and declare himself willing to bare arms in the defence of his hearth and home. The men who have already enrolled comprise of representatives of the professional, business and artisan classes and they are ready to work shoulder to shoulder for the benefit of their country.*

The *Western Times* of 19 June reported that the Devon and Cornwall Branch of the National Poor Law Officers' Association was held at the Exeter City Workhouse, presided over by Mr E. Birch of Devonport. He said that it wasn't just sufficient to relieve poverty but to find the cause of it. He spoke of the hardship felt by soldiers and their families. The paper reported:

> *Even this week, he had heard of a case in Plymouth where a soldier had returned from the front wounded, had been discharged from hospital recovered, but had been discharged from the Army as unfit for further service and was in great need for himself his wife and children.*

He went on to say: 'There will be thousands of such cases when the war is over and it is for the officers entrusted with the duties of relieving the poor and needy to speedily consider this subject and formulate some scheme which would be of a national service and a blessing to mankind.'

As the Battle of the Somme raged in Europe, relatives back in Exeter dreaded a knock on the door, as they had throughout the war, of the telegram boy bringing news of their loved ones' deaths. Newspapers carried the news of all wounded and killed soldiers.

The death columns of the local newspapers provided a pointer to the extent of the tragedies of Jutland and of the first battle of the Somme. An eye-witness reported:

We passed along the line of German ships some miles away. The air was heavy with masses of smoke black, yellow, green, of every colour, which drifted between the opposing lines. Again and again salvoes of shells fell short of the mark. I watched the Iron Duke swinging through the seas, letting off broadside after broadside, wicked tongues of flames leaping through clouds of smoke. The din of battle was stunning, stupendous, deafening, as hundreds of the heaviest guns in the world gave tongue at once. All (officers) on board the Indefatigable, the Defence and the Black Prince were lost; only four of the Queen Mary and two of the Invincible were saved. The list of (officers) killed numbers 333, and included Rear Admirals Hood and Arbuthnot, whose flags were carried on the Invincible and Defence respectively.

Entertainment continued in the city and on Tuesday 25 July, the *Exeter and Plymouth Gazette* announced 'an exciting drama' at the Palladium. The article read:

For the first three days of the present week, the management of the Exeter Palladium, Paris Street, have secured an exceptionally fine cinematograph film to 'top' a programme which should amply satisfy the most exacting patron. The title, 'Paste', conveys little of the thrilling nature of the picture. It is produced in four lengthy reels and the story, by Bannister Merwin, is a drama which gives plenty of scope for M Henri De Vries, a well-known cinema artiste, to display his histrionic ability. The plot deals with the substitution of a paste gem for a diamond pendant, the exciting episodes connected therewith being portrayed in a realistic manner. A spool of special interest to West of England folk is 'Wonderful Wessex' while the comic element is much to the fore in 'Max joins the Colours' and 'Ready for Reno.' The Pathe Gazette has become so popular that it needs no further commendation to the public.

In August, the 2nd (Home Service) Garrison Battalion, which had been

A cartoon in the **Devon and Exeter Gazette** *of Friday 25 August 1916, which appeared under the headline 'The Enemy in our Camp'. The caption read: 'The Board of Trade ha[s] now the power to take decisive action against those who withhold corn, flo[ur] and meat for the purpose of obtaining higher prices.'*

formed in Exeter in June 1916, moved to Plymouth and Falmouth becoming the 5th Battalion of the Royal Defence Corps.

The *Western Times* of 15 August reported the case of a discharged soldier who was charged with failure to produce his registration card. The story read:

> *At the Exeter Police Court on Friday, an engine driver, of no fixed address, named Reginald Charles Osmond, was charged with failing to produce his registration card. PC Blackmore visited a lodging house in Smythen Street on Thursday and found the man in bed. He was unable to produce a certificate and said that he did not know anything about it. Inspector Martin said the man had an Army discharge certificate. He had served for 89 days and had been discharged as unfit for service. He was not likely to be called up for medical re-examination. Osmond was of dull intellect and no doubt his statement that he was ignorant of the necessity of having a registration card was correct. Accused, who said he was subject to fits, was dismissed and was recommended to apply to the local authorities for a card.*

On Tuesday 15 August and Wednesday 16 August, Lord John Sanger's All-British Royal Circus and Menagerie was held in a field near the tram terminus in Pinhoe Road, Exeter. It had been seven years since Sanger's Circus had last visited the city and their return was much looked forward to. Amongst the important additions to the circus was a troupe of Russian Cossacks advertised as 'brave soldiers of the Czar who have done such noble work during the present war'. The Cossacks, who were barred from fighting in the war, planned to show Exonians their skill at horse-riding for which they were famed. This included

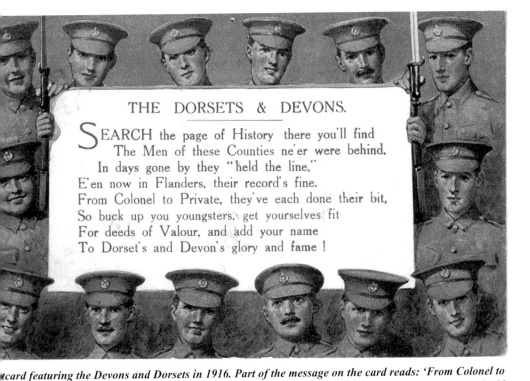

THE DORSETS & DEVONS.

SEARCH the page of History there you'll find
     The Men of these Counties ne'er were behind.
  In days gone by they "held the line,"
E'en now in Flanders, their record's fine.
From Colonel to Private, they've each done their bit,
So buck up you youngsters, get yourselves fit
For deeds of Valour, and add your name
To Dorset's and Devon's glory and fame !

*card featuring the Devons and Dorsets in 1916. Part of the message on the card reads: 'From Colonel to
e, they've each done their bit, so buck up you youngsters and get yourself fit, for deeds of Valour and add
name, to Dorset's and Devon's glory and fame!'*

jumping from one horse to another while at full gallop. Other acts
included 'the beautiful Della Cassa Sisters', who gave an exhibition
with horses and elephants.

The *Western Times* reported:

*Sanger's pure white twin horses are introduced by Francesca in an
exhibition of high school riding and driving. Sea lions take part in
the greatest animal act in the world; it is a truly marvellous
exhibition. The Aerial Danes may be expected to give a most thrilling
performance. There will be two performances, one at 3pm and the
other at 8pm and the prices of admission are popular.*

The *Western Times* of Thursday 17 August reported that an old boy of
St John's Hospital School, Exeter, Private Arthur Henry Herbert
Procter, had been awarded the Victoria Cross by the King whilst on a
visit to the Western Front. Private Procter of the King's Liverpool
Regiment, Territorial Force, was quoted as saying, 'I have never been
funky before the Boche but I was nervous at having to face the King.'

The *Western Times* of Friday 1 September told the story of a near
fatal event for a 9-year-old boy called Jack Widgery of Longbrook

On Friday 1 September 1916, the Western Times *published a photo of 'Devon Lads Who Are Thinking of Home'. The caption beneath it read:* 'I used to be agent for the Western Times at Morchard Bishop,' writes Pte J Ford, in sending us the above photo of Devon men who are getting ready to put the finishing touches to the Huns, 'and as your popular paper is so widely read, we thought our friends at home would like to see how well and happy we look!' The men are, reading from left to right:- Back row: R H Eynon (Plymouth), S B Baten (St Thomas, Exeter), C Stone (Ide, Exeter), B Kiff (Combemartin). Next row: T Glanfield (Exeter), A Bowden (Exeter), A England (Coombe Pyne), G Glanville (Lifton), J Cullwick (Exeter), C J Jerrett (Exeter), A H Driver (Beer), W Ridge (Heanton Punchardon), Lanham (Southampton). Second row: C Snow (Bovey Tracey), T D Tolley (Bovey Tracey), Sergt Basey (Durham), J Kitson (Exeter), C F Medland (Plymouth). Kneeling: G Brooks (Dawlish), J Ford (Morchard Bishop), C C Short (Hartland), J Ball (Silverton), R Quance (Plymouth), A Blanchard (Barnstaple), W Minhenick (Plymouth).

Street, Exeter. The boy had been fishing for minnows with other boys under the iron bridge. At one point he fell into the water and nearly drowned. He was saved by an 11-year-old companion, who grabbed a stake with one hand and waded out in the water until it was chest height. With his other hand, he grabbed Widgery and kept his head above water until the arrival of Special Constable Rousham, who managed to pull them both to safety. Widgery was said to be little the worse for his immersion.

On 9 September, *the Exeter and Plymouth Gazette* reported the news of the formation on the Cadet Brigade. The story read:

An advertisement in another column gives a first list of the

In the **Western Times** *of Friday 8 September 1916, under the headline 'Devon Men Mean Business', appeared a photo of troops overseas. The accompanying story read: 'We are not allowed to say where this photograph was taken, except that it was taken 'somewhere' where the spirit of 'up-and-at-'em' prevails. As you can guess from their up-turned sleeves, these brave Devon lads mean business. From left to right they are:- In the doorway: Pte P Anger (Exeter) and Pte Huxtable (Barnstaple). Standing: Ptes C Levett (Tiverton), R C Hurford (Exeter), Skinner (Exeter), Jenkins (Plymouth), F Plymsell (Exeter), A Madge (Exeter), T Hill (Torquay), L Madge (Crediton), F Notley (Exeter) and E Nicks (Exeter). Sitting:- Back row: Pte F Reynolds (Starcross), Pte C Knowles (Bradninch), Cpl L Hedger (Exeter), Pte H Hillman (Exeter). Second row: Pte G Melhuish (Exeter), Pte G Wedlake (Starcross), Pte A Ford (Exeter), Lce-Cpl Dimond (Dartmouth), Pte C Saunders (Exeter), Pte R Grant (Exmouth). Front row: Pte Winter (Torquay), Pte F Adams (Plymouth), Private L Tregale (Exeter) and Pte J Southcott (Exeter).'*

subscriptions received by the Reverend H de Vere Welchman towards the Equipment Fund of the Exeter Cadet Battalion. A capital start has been made towards securing the £450 required. The Battalion is open to all boys in business houses and works, apprentices, office, errand, tram and school boys. Mr Welchman is organising the thing thoroughly and, as it should be, seeing that the Battalion is affiliated to the 4th Battalion Devon Regiment, with all the honours attaching to it, and seeing that the Cathedral School Cadet Company is fourth among the Cadet units of Great Britain. So every candidate has to show on his application form the signature of a parent as evidence of approval and of the schoolmaster or employer as evidence of good character. The Battalion is to have the use of the Territorial RE Drill Hall in Colleton Crescent. Already applications have been made from almost 300 eligible boys for membership and more are coming in. But very few of the boys are in a position to provide their own uniforms and Mr Welchman's appeal is for £450 to cover equipment and other initial expenses. The promoters feel that the movement that they are encouraging is one destined to prove a real and lasting gain to the city of Exeter and to the country as well as to the boys themselves. The appeal is signed by Mr Joseph Gould, Cadet Captains E S Plummer, Arthur C Reed, Charles J Ross and H de Vere Welchman.

For two days, a film entitled *The Battle of the Somme* was shown at the Empire and the Palladium. The film had previously been seen by the King and Queen who stated: 'The public should see these pictures that they may have some idea of what the Army is doing and what war means.'

The *Western Morning News* reported:

The whole film is extremely well arranged, the various details being pieced together in their proper sequence, so that a splendid sight can be obtained of the magnificent and heroic, but awful, events which transpired on that eventful first of July when the lads of the Empire swarmed over the parapet and commenced that tremendous push which, to a greater or lesser extent, has continued up to the present and is still being driven home. The great artillery preparations for the advance are shown in much detail; the heavy guns belching forth destruction against the German trenches; the infantry and other branches of the Army, in perfect order, taking up positions of readiness for the advance.

The film will be especially interesting to West country men for it shows something of what our gallant Devon and Cornwall lads did. In this connection a pretty little domestic touch is given to the grimness of the battle picture by the portion of the film which depicts the Devons receiving parcels, letters etc. from the dear old homeland while the battle is still in progress. The eagerness with which the men seize hold of the letter bearing the familiar handwriting or carry off the parcel prepared with loving care in dear old 'Blighty' serves to remind those at home how much our brave lads cherish those links with those they have left behind at their country's call.

Yesterday, large crowds visited the Empire and Palladium each time the film was shown and we advise all who wish to see it to book seats for the remaining performances without delay.

On 24 September, troops from the New Zealand Expeditionary Force arrived in Plymouth en route to Salisbury Plain. On leaving Plymouth's Friary Lane Station, they were told that food would be laid on for them at their first stop at Exeter Central. However, the train stopped at the Bere Ferrers Station and troops alighted the train from the wrong side straight onto the tracks. They fell straight into the path of the London Waterloo to Plymouth Express and nine men were killed instantly. All were later buried at Efford Cemetery with military honours.

On Friday 29 September, the *Western Times* reported that Lieutenant Ernest Gould, ASC, of Exeter had been appointed officer-in-charge of a section of caterpillar tractors and would shortly proceed to the Front.

Meanwhile, back home, all electric globes at Exeter Cathedral had been supplied with shades to comply with the lighting order.

In the same newspaper, the death of a young soldier was reported. It read:

News reached Exeter on Tuesday of the death of Lieutenant P J Cole, eldest son of Mr and Mrs J Cole, of Chittlehampton. Deceased, who was about 26 years of age, was an exceedingly smart officer. Formerly in the North Devon Hussars, he transferred to the Territorial Artillery and was stationed some time at Exeter. Later, he was at Salisbury Plain and proceeded to the Western front where, a few days ago, he was wounded in the thigh and groin. A telegram was received by his friends at home that he had been seriously, though not dangerously wounded, but he succumbed to his injuries two days later. He was engaged to Miss Oliver of Powderham Crescent, Exeter, daughter of Mrs W H Oliver and niece of Mr A T Oliver, and had many friends in the city and neighbourhood as well as in North Devon.

On Thursday 12 October, a presentation was made at the Exeter Police

Members of the Devons in a rest camp pictured in October 1916. The picture features: Back row: Driver W. Isaacs, Trooper J. Honeybun, Pte A. H. Williams, Driver W. Lear. Sitting: Pte E. Pensford, Second Corpl E. S. Shortridge, Lance-Corpl W. R. Day, Lance-Corpl J. S. Maddock, Sergt C. Burridge, the Rev S. L. Webb, Ptes E. Bickle, N. J. Cobley, W. H. Shute, J. Burgess. Front row: Pte H. E. Bengey, Sapper R. Prowse, Pte S. Roberts.

Court by the mayor, Mr J. G. Owen, on behalf of the Royal Humane Society, to Thomas Trump of Coombe Street. Trump, aged 47 and a warehouseman, saved the life of a 12½-year-old boy, Leonard Philip Baker, who had fallen into the River Exe on 8 August. The mayor stated that the boy was walking along the quay when he fell into 10 feet of water. Trump, who was a distance away, ran to the spot and rescued the boy while still wearing his clothes and boots. Once rescued, the boy was exhausted and unable to speak. Six weeks beforehand, Trump had also rescued another boy who had fallen into the water. For his conduct then, he was written a letter of thanks from the chief constable.

The *Western Times* of Friday 13 October reported on the sixtieth sitting of the Exeter Tribunal, whose job it was to decide who should be exempt from the army. During the proceedings, they dealt with their 2,000th case. The previous day's batch of cases had numbered more than forty and were presided over by the mayor (Mr J. G. Owen) and

Mr C. J. Ross representing the military.

Amongst the cases heard were:

- E. R. Daniel, aged 32, a gun and rifle repairer who had his appeal for exemption applied for by Messrs J. Webber and Sons. The tribunal heard that a partner and ten men from the firm had already joined the colours. Further exemption was refused.

A cartoon appeared in the **Exeter and Plymouth Gazette** *on Friday 13 October 1916 under the headline 'Darkest Exeter'. The caption underneath read: 'The members of the Committee appointed to find a Mayor, being business men and, presumably having to devote their evenings to the quest, will find their difficulties increased owing to the lighting regulations.'*

- Mr A. .L Honey, a chartered accountant, applied for F. F. Coles, aged 37, an audit clerk holding a confidential position. The staff at the firm were already half what they were due to the war. Exemption was extended until 31 January.

- Mr C. M. Silver for E. F. Doidge, aged 25, described as a dental mechanic and the only man employed by him. Exemption was again granted until 31 January.

Other people appealing for exemption included bootmakers, plumbers, dairymen, ironmongers, bakers, car mechanics, coach builders and bookbinders. Some cases were allowed exemption for a short period on health grounds or for carrying out essential work.

A Mr Almy represented Francis Elliott, skipper and owner of a fishing boat who had been declared C2. He also represented his brother. The newspaper reported:

On the last occasion, the Tribunal suggested that the men should join the R.N.V.R. but on presenting himself, he was not accepted as he had not been rejected for military service. As they were unable to carry out their obligations to the Tribunal, they asked for a re-hearing. He suggested that applicant should be granted exemption conditional on his joining the R.N.V.R.

Mr E H Sermon: Is not that what we did?

Mr Almy: Not exactly and the result is that they fall between two stools.

Mr Sermon: They would be more use to the Navy that the Army.

Mr Almy: Obviously. The younger brother then tried to take the bull by the horns and get into the Navy direct but was rejected entirely by Dr Woore.

In answer to Alderman Cumming, Mr Almy said that the military doctors passed him for general service while the naval doctor rejected him altogether. He thought if the military wanted him, he should be given a chance of re-examination by the military board in London.

Colonel Stovell said that he had suggested to Major Kendall that he should go before the new Medical Board at Exeter but he had not received a reply yet.

Alderman Cumming said that he thought the man should have a re-examination but it was agreed to leave this over until the case came before the Tribunal next week and in the case of the present application, exemption to December 1st was confirmed.

In the case of Charles Strawbridge, fish salesman, wholesale buyer and licensee of the Cary Arms, the Recruiting Officer recommended exemption until 1st December.

Mr Almy (for the applicant): He is in the public-house in the evening, when he cannot buy fish.

Colonel Stovell: Don't people want drink in the morning?

Mr Almy asked for the exemption for a period of Francis H L Drake, employed as a carter in the postal service. He wanted exemption until after the Christmas trade, on the grounds of public convenience.

Colonel Stovell referred to a letter in The Times, the writer saying: 'On my way to England, I stayed a night in Berlin. The chief changes to be noticed in the capital were the lessened number of vehicles in the streets and the number of women employed. There were women workers at the station, women in charge of the tramcars, women delivered telegrams and letters and even drove the postal vans.'

Mr Almy: I hope we will not take Berlin as an example of what we should do.

Colonel Stovell: In some ways we might copy them.

It was pointed out that Drake was a young man, 22 years of age, and exemption was granted until 1st December without leave to appeal.

On 9 November, the *Western Times* carried a story about a letter received from New Zealand at the Mayoress's Depot. It read:

Dear Madam,

I am in receipt of a letter from my son who has left New Zealand to join the forces. His letter is full of praise for beautiful Devon, about the lovely fields and hedges, and about the ladies in the fields haymaking, and dozens of other things his dad has told him about dear old England. Among other matters is this sentence, 'Oh, dad, the Mayoress of Exeter and the ladies assisting her was just bosker; she was at the station and gave the boys a cup of tea, cakes and buns etc. and my word it was acceptable.' My wife was forced to cough to keep the tears away as I read it out and we both said, 'Well done, Exeter.' It's these little acts of kindness by the ladies of dear old England that makes the eyes of the fathers and mothers of New Zealand feel damp, especially when our first lad has given his life for the Empire and the wound is very sore yet. The lad you handed a cup of tea, threw up a beautiful 250 acre farm to come home and do his bit and it's the meeting of such little acts of kindness that heeps to hearten up the brave fellows that are travelling of miles to fight for our beloved country. Would you accept the thanks of my wife and myself for the cup of tea handed to our lad and when next time we visit old England, we will make a point of thanking you in person. Meanwhile, three cheers for the ladies of Exeter were given quite lustily in Roto-o-rangi and the trees in the bush bent their branches and answered quite plainly 'Amen.'

Yours faithfully, on behalf of the lad's mother and myself, Frank Paine.

An appeal was issued in the *Western Times* of Wednesday 15 November. It read:

> *In order that Christmas may be made enjoyable for the wounded soldiers who are being cared for in Devon hospitals, an appeal is again issued by the Committee in charge of raising the necessary fund. Mr Charles J Ross (the chairman) states that this year they anticipate meeting the requirements of close on a thousand wounded. To provide for every wounded man in all the civil, military and VAO hospitals a suitable gift, in addition to the usual dainties, quite £400 will be necessary, whilst taking into account enhanced prices, £500 will not be too much. Something of utility, pocket knives, pencil cases, pipes, besides donations in money, gifts in kind, cakes and fruit, all will be most acceptable and welcome. There will be a depot in St Sidwell's, Exeter, where everything will be taken in, arranged and stored.*

On Thursday 21 December, the *Exeter and Plymouth Gazette* announced that Mrs W. E. Carter of 27 Polsloe Road had been notified that her eldest son, Mr G. S. B. Carter, a captain in the Royal Mail company, was killed at sea on 8 December. The ship he was on, a steamer, was torpedoed without warning and everyone on board, apart

On 2 December 1916, the **Exeter and Plymouth Gazette** *announced that Deller's Café would be closing and moving to a new address at Bedford Street.*

DELLER'S CAFE.

THE ABOVE CAFE

WILL BE CLOSED

THE WHOLE OF

MONDAY NEXT,

AND A

TEMPORARY CAFE

WILL BE OPENED IN THE

New Premises, BEDFORD STREET,

On TUESDAY MORNING.

An advert for **Cinderella,** *the pantomime in Exeter for 1916. The show opened at the Theatre Royal on Monday 25 December.*

from those on the raft section, were killed. The steamship was on fire for two days before it burnt itself out before sinking. The newspaper reported that Mr Carter was 42 and was well-liked and respected in Exeter. His brother, Mr C. H. Carter, was an assistant solicitor to Devon County Council.

Towards Christmas, the committee of the Royal Devon and Exeter Hospital appealed for gifts from the public. They stated that books, rabbits, game and vegetables were urgently needed.

A lighting order was issued before Christmas stating that vehicle lamps were to be lit at 4.35pm and shops and house lights were to be obscured at 6.05pm.

On the week commencing Monday 25 December, the 28th annual Christmas pantomime opened at the Theatre Royal featuring an old favourite, *Cinderella*. It was very warmly received and include something for all ages. Mr George Thorne, a well-known Savoy comedian, played the baron while the principal boy was played by Miss Molly Butler who, newspaper revues noted, 'makes a charming Prince'. Cinderella was played by Hilda Denton, who was said to have a sweet soprano voice. Miss Dorothy Rosevear played a dashing Dandini and her song *Every girl has a Tommy somewhere* was one of the hits of the pantomime. The ugly sisters were played by Mr Arthur Louville and Miss Winifred Fairlie, who was described as an excellent impressionist copying the voices of Caruso, George Formby, Yvette Gilbert and Harry Lauder.

The *Western Times* of 30 December told the tale of a young deserter. The story read:

> *A young man of fine physique, Robert Harland, a merchant seaman, was charged on remand at Exeter Police Court yesterday with being an absentee from the Army. The Chief Constable informed the Bench that Harland was found at a lodging house without a registration card. He said that he was a merchant seaman, and it was proved that he was so, but it was also clear that he joined a ship at London, sailed to Dartmouth, and then deserted the ship. The Chief Constable submitted that the defendant having deserted his ship became liable to serve with the Colours. Defendant told the Bench that he had always been a seaman and that if he had to join the Colours, he should prefer the Navy. The Chairman (Mr J Stocker): You can enter into those explanations at the Barracks. You will be handed over to the military authorities.*

CHAPTER FOUR

1917 – Seeing it through

On Sunday 28 January, a meeting of the A and B companies of the 1st Exeter Battalion Devonshire Volunteer Regiment was held at the headquarters, St James' Park, Exeter. They discussed the official regulations from the War Office, which stated that specially trained sections of the volunteer force would be formed for service in the event of an invasion being imminent. Colonel Richards, the officer in command of the battalion, expressed the hope that all who were able would join Section A (men over military age) or Section B (men of military age).

John Taylor of 6 Bridge Street, Exeter, found himself at Exeter's police court for failing to obscure a light burning in a garage at 17 Frog Street. The incident took place at 10.55pm and was reported by PS Wreford. The defendant was found guilty and fined five shillings.

Other cases heard included that of William Henry Balkwill, who was fined five shillings for riding a motor cycle in Cowley Bridge Road at 7.55pm whilst using an acetylene lamp that didn't have the front glass obscured. George Cooper of Graslawn, Exeter, was also fined five shillings for 'driving a horse and van without a rear light'.

On 1 March, the *Exeter and Plymouth Gazette* reported on entertainment in Exeter and their story featured a visiting mind reader. Under the headline, 'For Church Army Huts', the article read:

> *In our advertising columns will be found particulars of Mr Alfred Capper's interesting and unique entertainment, comprising experiments in thought-transmission and other mysterious*

phenomena, which he is giving next Thursday afternoon and evening, March 8th, in the Barnfield, Exeter, in aid of the Church Army Recreation Huts for the troops on the Western front. Mr Capper has given his entertainment at Windsor Castle, Marlborough House and in all parts of the world. Recent entertainments by him at the Aeolian Hall, London and at Brighton have realised more than £600 for the Church Army Huts and crowded audiences have testified alike to the unusual interest of the entertainment and the excellence of the object which Mr Capper is promoting. We have no doubt that there will be a full house to witness the entertainment next week and the result will be a substantial benefit to the Church Army Hut Fund. This Society has already hundreds of recreation huts at home and in every theatre of war and there is an incessant demand for more of them. Our lads at the Front are enduring much hardship, and even suffering, and it is up to us at home to do all we can to give them comfort and recreation in their off-duty hours.

At the beginning of March, the *Exeter and Plymouth Gazette* wrote of a contribution received. The article read:

British bicycle troops at Brie, Somme, March 1917.

Colonel Savile, of Barley, Exeter, writing from the battle front, to Mr G A Drake, manager of the Union of London and Smiths Bank, Exeter, says that he sees by the Devon and Exeter Gazette that the Farthing Breakfast Fund, of which Mr Drake is treasurer, is in want of money and expresses the pleasure it gives him to send a cheque for £2 2s. The Colonel's kindly thought for the poor children of the city will be very greatly appreciated.

tram crash in 1917. The first serious accident since the inauguration of the Exeter electric tramway stem in 1904 took place on Wednesday 7 March 1917. One woman was killed and five others were injured, ith three requiring hospital treatment. It left the rails at the bottom of Bridge Street by Bonhay and ommercial Roads before skidding and turning over with a loud crash. The tramcar was driven by Charles anders, age 42, who had only recently been employed by the corporation.

On 8 March, Exeter City Council announced that they had not been able to obtain sufficient land to meet the demand for allotments. They decided to set aside an acre of land at Gras Lawn to be used. The land had previously been bought by the council for the erection of the

Cottage Hostel. The area formed the northern end of the college playing field not far from the district of St Leonard's. Altogether, the council had been able to grant 140 allotments covering a total of 9 acres.

On 24 March, the *Yellowstone News* in Montana carried the headline 'U.S. expected to announce that state of war exists'. The newspaper went on to report 'News received from Plymouth that fifteen men, some of them Americans, had been drowned when the American merchantmen *Vigilancia* was sunk without warning by a German submarine'. The story also stated that 'President Wilson is expected, within 48 hours, to indicate definitely that he believes a virtual state of war exists between the United States and Germany'.

On 5 April, the *Evening Herald* reported:

> *The U.S. Senate has passed the resolution declaring a state of war with Germany by 82 votes to 6 at 11.15pm after 13 hours continuous debate. There was no demonstration when the result was announced.*

America joined the war on 6 April, 1917.

The *Exeter and Plymouth Gazette* of Saturday 14 April featured an article about Exeter's boy cadets. It read:

> *Considerable interest was aroused in Exeter, last evening, when the Exeter Cadet Corps, which was formed recently, celebrated Mesopotamia Day by holding its first march through the city. The Corps is affiliated to the 1/4th Battalion of the Devon Regiment, a fact of which they are proud. Some 370 strong in all, the Corps last evening paraded at the headquarters, The Friars. They represented the number who had been fitted with uniforms. Some thirty or forty more uniforms are available and will be served out as early as possible.*
>
> *Lieut. A.R. Palmer was in charge of the Fife and Drum Band and Bugle-Major Hawkes directed the Bugle Band. Also present were various officers including Captain the Rev. H. de Vere Welchman.*
>
> *Previous to the march-out, the Corps engaged in brief evolutions at the Drill Hall.*
>
> *A request had been made that the public should support the march by displaying flags and otherwise manifesting interest in the event. This was done. At headquarters, a large crowd congregated including a good number of the juvenile element. Numerous*

spectators also lined the approaches to The Friars and Holloway Street. Shortly after 7.30, the Corps lined up and, headed by the two bands, marched smartly off. All along the route, much interest was shown in the Cadets and, at the junction of High Street and Queen Street, the crowd assumed large proportions. On all sides, it was agreed, the lads shaped very well for a first march. It was quite an inspiration to see the diminutive members, nearly all cap, belt and puttee, marching proudly along and keeping step with the band like seasoned veterans. The turn-out proved very successful and had a good augury for the future of the Corps. As the Corps passed the Guildhall, the Deputy-Mayor (Mr Bradley Rowe) took the salute. When the lads had returned to the Drill Hall, the officer in command eulogised their steadiness on parade. He thanked all those who had kindly supported the movement. Lieut. Palmer and Bugle-Major Hawkes for the excellent services rendered by the bands, Messrs. J. and G. Ross for the manner in which they had carried out the supplying of the uniforms and Sergt.-Major Aplin for his untiring

Anzac day in Exeter on 25 April 1917. The **Western Times** *announced Anzac Day as 'the anniversary of the tragically splendid day when the Australian and New Zealand troops gained imperishable glory on the Gallipoli Peninsula'. The event commenced with a morning service at the cathedral that was followed by the Anzacs marching to the Guildhall. In the afternoon, entertainment was provided at Hele's School organised by Mr Snowball, who was a representative of Australian Soldiers' Societies.*

efforts in instructing the Cadets. The parade concluded with cheers for the King, Capt. de Vere Welchman and others.

On 25 April, the *Exeter and Plymouth Gazette* announced the proceeds of Primrose Day. Altogether a total of £144 had been raised for the Red Cross.

The 'Our Letters' section of the *Western Times* of Monday 7 May featured an appeal headed 'Hospitality Wanted For Australian Soldiers'. The letter read:

To the Editor of The Western Times.

Sir, – We are all very proud of the brave deeds of our Australian troops at the front. Many of them have been on this side two years or more and have no friends in this country. When they get short leave from the front, there is no home life possible for them; they can merely go to London and London without a friend is a very lonely place. Canon McLaren and I have on several occasions entertained Australian soldiers on leave and a very delightful experience it has been. We are now asked by the Australian Comforts Fund Committee whether it is possible to obtain invitations for more of them and I am writing to say that if there are any households in

Percy Roberts and Catherine Roberts of the Exeter Army Pay Department boating at Exeter in 1917.

Exeter, and Devonshire generally, prepared to entertain an Australian soldier back from the battlefield on leave for a few days, I shall be glad to hear from them.

Yours sincerely,
Elsie McLaren.
The Close, Exeter, May 5 1917.

The Mayor of Exeter's Forget-Me-Not-Day appeal at Teignmouth. On Friday 18 May 1917, 30,000 forget-me-nots were on sale at Exeter as part of the city's effort for the Hospitality Fund. The minimum price for souvenirs was one penny and sixpence for a spray. Forget-me-not days also became popular in other towns and villages around the country and were held in Exeter for several years in support of the troops.

On Friday 18 May, the *Western Times* published a request from the director-general of voluntary organisations to all working parties that assist the Mayoress of Exeter's Depot. The request urged the necessity of voluntary workers to prepare woollens, etc, for soldiers for the following winter. The letter read:

For the guidance of your committee, I am to add that it is anticipated that all knitted comforts will be required in large and increasing quantities in the Autumn and it is hoped that the assistance of all workers will be enlisted as to ensure an adequate stock of such comforts being available for dispatch overseas to the distant theatres of war in August and to the Western front at the beginning of October.

The *Exeter and Plymouth Gazette* of Saturday 16 June announced the 'Summer Time Lighting'. Vehicle lamps were to be lit at 10pm and shop and house lights were to be obscured at 11.30pm.

On the grass at St Luke's, Exeter in 1917. Shown in the photo is Percy Lawrence Roberts and his w... Catherine Ethel Roberts, who met during the First World War whilst working in the Army Pay Departm... in Exeter. Percy Roberts was 22 at the outbreak of the war but wasn't deemed fit for active service.

With many fathers killed or away fighting in the war, many children found themselves before the local magistrates. On 9 July, the *Exeter and Plymouth Gazette* reported on the proceedings at the Exeter Juvenile Court. The report read:

Yesterday, at the Exeter Juvenile Court, before Messrs. P. Kelland (in the chair), H. Hall, H. J. Munro and J. Stokes, a 12-year-old lad was summoned for doing damage to 23 lime trees during the month of March in Willey's Avenue, to the value of 20s, the property of the Exeter City Council. Defendant pleaded guilty to damaging eight trees. The lad said that he was very sorry. He had been before the Bench once previously for throwing stones. Fined 2s 6d and 2s 6d towards the damage.

Two lads, aged 13 years, were summoned for stealing fruit, value 2d, from a nursery in Tan Lane on 29th June, the property of Mr F. Cosham. Both pleaded guilty. Mr Cosham found four apples on one lad and a quantity of strawberries on the other. One of the defendants had previously been before the Bench three times and the other, once. Each was fined 5s.

Another lad, aged 9 years, was summoned for stealing a packet of dry fruit, value 3½d. He pleaded guilty and was fined 2s.

Three other lads, aged 13 to 15 years, were summoned for committing malicious damage to fruit trees on the 4th inst. Each defendant pleaded guilty. They were seen throwing stones at the trees and, when caught, two denied the offence and the other admitted it. One of the lads stated that the fruit was tempting and that was why he threw the stones. The lad who admitted the offence when caught was fined 1s and 2s 6d towards the damage; the others were ordered to pay 2s 6d fine and 2s 6d each towards the damage.

Five other lads, aged 9 to 13 years, pleaded guilty to stealing a quantity of gooseberries, value 2s. from a fruit garden at Whipton, the property of Mr Hill. This was the first time that either had been before the Bench. The Chief Constable (Mr A. F. Nicholson) stated it was not only the loss of fruit but the damage done by climbing over the hedges and crossing the beds. Each defendant was fined 2s, Mr Hill stating he would not ask for any damages.

A 14-year-old errand boy was charged with stealing, during the past six weeks, a 'Bradshaw' Railway Guide, value 1s, the property of Messrs. Wheaton and Co., the lad's employers. He was also charged with stealing a parcel of examination papers and answers, value 7s 10d, also the property of Messrs. Wheaton and Co. The Chief Constable said the lad sold the railway guide to a lady for 10d after telling her a pitiful story. He disposed of the examination papers, with a mallet, to a soldier for 1s. The mother of the lad stated that she had had a lot of trouble with the defendant and an elder son. Detective Edwards stated that the elder lad never went to work and this lad had a very bad record. He was very untruthful and had been before the Bench three times previously. The magistrates decided to send the lad to a Reformatory for five years, the parents to pay 1s weekly towards his maintenance.

The *Exeter and Plymouth Gazette* of Tuesday 10 July reported the inquest of an Exeter girl who had been killed on the railway. Hilda Jane Millicent Barnes, aged 16, was the daughter of Edward Barnes, a railway porter on the London and South Western Railway. She was found on the line on the previous Saturday. Her sister, Florence Mabel Barnes, said that she left the house at 8.15pm on Friday evening, saying that she was going to the cinema or for a trip on the river. She said that she was going to meet an 'army pay corps fellow' whom she'd first met a week earlier.

PC W. T. Fewins stated that on Saturday morning, at about 3.20am, a report had come from a ganger that a body had been found below the bridge at Stafford Bridge.

Time off in 1917. Percy Roberts and Catherine Roberts (shown in the [worked in the Army Pay Department. In August 1915, St Luke's Tra College temporarily closed. Part of the building had already been giver to the Army Pay Office in January 1915 and it was felt that the buildin not big enough to accommodate the full complement of students requir the Board of Education.

Private Edward Harold Woodward testified that he had known the deceased since the previous Saturday when he had met her at about 9.15pm and had arranged to go for a walk the next day. He had met her twice since then and on the Friday had met her at 8.15pm on the corner of St James' Road. They went for a walk up to Old Tiverton Road and back to Cowley Bridge. On reaching the bridge, the deceased asked the time and on being told it was 10pm, she replied that her father would be very angry for stopping out so late. They hurried back and arrived at her home at 10.50pm, where she said that she was worried that her father would lock her out. She was afraid to go home so they wandered around and the soldier said that he would try to find her lodgings for the night. Private Woodward said that he tried for half-an-hour to persuade the girl to go home but she stated that she was afraid that if she stayed out all night that she would lose her reputation. Whilst wandering near the railway line, she said 'I shall do it!', meaning that she would commit suicide. She told the soldier that she had threatened to do this before when her father had become angry with her for staying out late. The soldier said that he left the deceased at the gate to the line between 1.30 and 2am and they arranged to go to the river the next evening.

The coroner asked the soldier if he thought she would return home after he left her, to which he replied, 'I thought she would.' The soldier said that he didn't take her threats of suicide seriously. He also stated that he did not know her age but assumed that she was about 18. He was 40 and married.

The foreman of the jury said that there was no evidence as to how the girl had got on the line and an open verdict was returned.

On Monday 16 July, Miss Buller, the administrator of the Exeter War Hospitals, made an appeal for support for performances of *A Tight Corner* at the Theatre Royal. The production was brought to the city by Captain A E Clayton, of the Depot Somerset LI, in aid of the Exeter War Hospitals. The *Exeter and Plymouth Gazette* reported that Captain Clayton and his colleagues had 'been doing splendid service by their clever amateur performances during the past few months and have in Somerset raised over £400 for various war funds'.

The *Exeter and Plymouth Gazette* of Tuesday 17 July announced 'Ten Tommies at Exeter Hippodrome.' The article read:

The 110 Wilts group with some of the Dorsets at the Exeter Army Pay Offices.

The Ten Tommies, who are the premier turn at the Exeter Hippodrome this week, cannot fail to give complete satisfaction to patrons of this popular house of amusement. Every member of the company has fought gallantly for his country and been wounded in France, Gallipoli, Egypt or Salonica. Their entertainment abounds in humour and talent and, from the start to finish, there is not a dull moment. The song by one of the party, 'When our lads in khaki get into Berlin' proves highly diverting while 'the boys' afford considerable amusement in a happy-go-lucky novelty, 'Sing, Boys, Sing.' They were accorded splendid receptions at both houses last night. It was announced, prior to the turn, that the personal discharge certificate of each man was in the possession of the management and could be seen by anyone interested on application. Booklets giving a few details of the men are on sale and the proceeds will go towards the War Seal Foundation which is erecting specially-designed dwellings for disabled soldiers and sailors. Exonians should make a point of paying a visit during the week and thus show their appreciation of the 'lads in khaki' who have done their bit for King and country in the present war.

The remainder of the programme is quite up to the standard for which the Hippodrome is noted. Described as the boy in white, Nan C Hearne is responsible for a very pleasing turn. Larry Lewis is a successful comedian and his quaint style creates much merriment. Fred Powell and Co (including John Brittain) appear in an original and quaintly humorous character comedy skit entitled 'Getting the dinner in.' It is a very entertaining turn. Violet Stockelle, a charming comedienne, is at once popular with her pretty songs which she renders in admirable style and dresses. Much amusement is afforded by the Milton Brothers as skating comedians, their performance also being one of great skill. A good all-round programme is completed by the excellent orchestral selections under the conductorship of Mr Joseph D Gabriel and the special war pictures on the Bioscope.

The 'Our Letters' section of the *Western Times* of Friday 20 July featured a request headed, 'An Appeal to Working Parties'. The letter read:

To the Editor of The Western Times.

Sir, – Socks and mufflers, but socks especially, will be required in as large or even larger numbers than before, for our troops at the front this autumn and winter. May I, therefore, urge the many working parties, and individual helpers, who have so generously helped the Mayoress's Depot in the past, to continue and, if possible, increase their efforts? We now have many Devon battalions at the front and in addition we receive urgent requests for bales from the Director-General of Voluntary Organisations. I am sure that it is hardly necessary to remind working parties that the Mayoress's Depot is permitted to supply wool from the War Office at cost price. It would greatly help us if we could hear from affiliated working parties the approximate quantities of wool they would wish reserved for them during the coming months. I shall be happy to hear from anyone desiring information on the matter.

Yours faithfully,
J. Kirk G. Owen, Mayoress.
The Guildhall, Exeter, July 18, 1917.

On Wednesday 15 August, a party of wounded troops from Nos 2 and 5 hospitals in Exeter were entertained on Teignmouth Pier by Mr and Mrs G. Hardy-Harris, Mrs Swettenham and friends. Joining them were injured soldiers from Newton VAO and Cottage Hospitals and the Teignmouth Hospital, making a total of 150 men. Competitions were indulged in including the egg and spoon race, bull board, deck quoits,

Competitors in the Exeter wounded soldiers angling contest during August 1917. Organisers and friends kept up a supply of bait and 'smokes'.

pig's eye and guessing the weight of the cake. Tea was laid on in the shore pavilion and afterwards, the party adjourned to the outer pavilion where a concert was given.

On Friday 17 August, the *Western Times* published a photo of wounded soldiers at Exeter taking part in an angling competition under the heading, 'Attacking on an Extended Front'.

On Friday 24 August, the funeral took place of Exeter airman,

Flight-Sergeant Arthur G. Rodgman, who was killed on the previous Monday evening at Wolvercote near Oxford. He was buried with full military honours at the Higher Cemetery, Exeter.

The Exeter and Plymouth Gazette reported:

Deceased, who was 22 years of age, was a son of Mr Rodgman of Port View. He was in an aeroplane at a height of 100 feet when smoke was observed and the machine fell blazing to the ground with a terrible crash. Rodgman was returning to Wolvercote when the accident happened. Deceased, who had been flying for five months, had been recommended for a commission in the Royal Flying Corps.

On Friday 7 September, the *Western Times* announced that an old Hele School boy had received a military honour. Corporal Hugh S. Taylor, of the Royal Canadian Regiment, who had been promoted to sergeant, was awarded the Military Medal for conspicuous bravery on the Western Front. He was also recommended for a commission in the Imperial Forces. He was the son of a former proprietor of the Elephant Inn, Exeter as well as being an old Hele School boy. Prior to enlistment, Sergeant Taylor had been employed as a telegraph operator in Melville, Saskatchewan. His parents had at one time lived in Winnipeg. Sergeant Taylor had been in the trenches continually since August 1915 and, with the exception of his captain, was the only original member of his company to escape injury.

On Thursday 11 October, the *Exeter and Plymouth Gazette* announced the upcoming entertainment at the Theatre Royal Exeter. Performed nightly, *Potash and Perlmutter* was 'a comedy of great human interest in three acts'. The advert announced that it had played for over 600 nights to crowded houses at the Queen's Theatre, London. Commencing on 15 October was a play described as the attraction of the season, *Betty* was a musical play and theatre-goers were advised to book early.

On Tuesday 16 October, the *Western Times* announced the death of Lieutenant-Colonel Sayres RAMC on the previous Wednesday. He had succumbed to wounds received at the Western Front during early July. Whilst in practice in Exeter, Sayres had been granted a commission in the 1st Wessex RAMC (TF). He was subsequently moved to Plymouth and soon after the outbreak of war was sent to the Front with one of the RAMC units and shortly after was promoted to the rank of lieutenant-colonel. He was said to be very popular with the men in his command. While serving at Ypres, he was injured when a shell burst close to him, which inflicted terrible injuries that caused him to lose his left leg, his right hand and one eye. He was said to have borne his affliction with much courage and cheerfulness and was greatly mourned by his friends and comrades within his unit.

On Friday 9 November, the *Western Times* published details about a military medal awarded to an Exeter postal official. Sapper Ernest Francis Radcliffe of A Signal Co, RE, whose home was at 45 Victor Street, Heavitree, was awarded the Military Medal for an act of gallantry while serving at the Western Front. On the night of 26 September, whilst near St Julien, he and Sapper Shear, another Exonian who also received a medal, were operating a signal lamp in a trench in the cemetery whilst under heavy shelling. He kept the lamp in operation until it was destroyed by a shell. Both men were partially buried in the trench and although badly shaken, Sapper Radcliffe and his comrade helped to maintain communication with a new lamp until they were relieved on the night of 27 September.

Before joining up, Sapper Radcliffe was a member of staff at Exeter's General Post Office.

On Tuesday 13 November, a well-known lecturer at the time, Gipsy Smith, visited Exeter and delivered an address at the Victoria Hall on the work of the YMCA in France and Flanders. Gipsy Smith had been connected with the work of the organisation on the Western Front for two years. There was great interest in his story and a huge crowd sought admission to the hall necessitating an overflow meeting.

The meeting was presided over by Mr W. H. Reed JP, the president of the local branch of the YMCA.

During the address, Gipsy Smith informed the audience that on the previous evening at Newport, £700 was raised in forty minutes for a hut to be known as 'The Newport Hut'. He asked for Exeter to do the same so that a hut could be called 'The Exeter Hut'.

The chairman immediately stated that he and Mrs Reed would be pleased to give £50 each and a little later, it was announced that they wished to add another £50 to the fund in memory of their son, Reverend Clifford Reed, who was killed while acting as chaplain at the Front. Mr E. S. Plummer, the honorary treasurer to the Exeter YMCA, said that he would give £100 while £50 was contributed by the Sheriff of Exeter and Mrs H. C. Rowe. Mr Rowe had had the misfortune to lose his sister while she was performing war work at the Front. He had another sister who was also rendering war services in France.

Other promises of £50 were made by the Reverend J F Sheldon, Mr Arthur Thomas and an anonymous contributor. Further gifts of £10 and £5 came in rapidly. A gift of 3d from a little boy with the message, 'All I've got,' drew from Gipsy Smith the remark, 'God bless you, my dear little chap.' A silver collection was taken at the main hall and also at the overflow meeting. The latter yielded £2 3s. The total amount raised came to £726 which, it was remarked, was well ahead of the total from the previous night's meeting at Newport.

Gipsy Smith thanked the donors in the name of the boys at the Front and all the workers of the YMCA who, he said, would appreciate to the full Exeter's splendid generosity.

The *Western Times* of Friday 30 November reported under the headline, 'Gallant Gunner at an Exeter VAD Hospital.' The story read:

Folkestone is not a little proud of the fact that one of its sons had

Nurses and staff at VA Hospital No 3 in 1917. VA 3 was situated in the City Hospital at Heavitree.

distinguished himself by a remarkable act of heroism. When at a hospital not far from the fighting at the Western Front, a badly wounded soldier was brought in. A doctor said the only chance of his life being saved was for somebody to allow his blood to be transferred to the wounded man's body. Gunner Fred Burvill at once volunteered and the transfer was effected. Following this 'gift of blood' secondary anaemia developed in the system of the donor who is now in hospital at Exeter. This young hero is the eldest son of Mr A Burvill of Hope Cottage, Black Bull Road, who for many years has been in the employ of successive Earls of Radnor as gardener. Gunner Burvill's brother, Sergeant H A Burvill, has just obtained a commission in the Worcestershire Regiment.

The *Derby Daily Telegraph* of Saturday 8 December reported that the eldest son of the Bishop of Exeter (Lord William Cecil) had been killed in action. Lieutenant Randle William Cecil was 28 years old and came over with the Canadian contingent before receiving a commission. The bishop had also previously lost another son in the war.

On Monday 10 December, the Exeter War Savings and War Economy Campaign was inaugurated with a ceremony attended by crowds of people. It was a cold, chilly day with the threat of snow but still the streets in the vicinity of Bedford Circus were crowded from an early hour. Throughout the afternoon, there was a stream of purchasers of War Bonds at the 'Tank', which was housed at the High Street entrance to Bedford Circus. The sides of the enclosure contained wreaths with evergreens and laurels. The central figure was the facsimile of a tank that had been designed by Lieutenant Thurgood, the

Exonians were encouraged to buy War Bonds at the Tank. A sign on the tank stated: 'The bonds bought here buy bombs and guns and build more tanks to beat the Huns.'

son of Mr and Mrs E. C. Thurgood of Exmouth. The tank was made in their garden by wounded soldiers convalescing at Exmouth hospitals. Lieutenant Thurgood was a section-commander in the Tank Corps and took part in the Battle of Arras. Adjoining the tank was an office where nine postal officials carried out the clerical work of the organisation.

Shortly before noon, the tank made its way through the streets, starting at Messrs Standfield and White's before proceeding up Sidwell Street and as far as the fountain before returning via High Street to North Street before returning back to Bedford Street. In front of the tank marched the Fife and Drum band of the Exeter Cadet Corps under the command of Bandmaster Palmer, with Lieutenant Knight marshalling the procession. The tank was pulled by a number of cadets while others manned the machine. A banner displayed on the tank stated: 'If you cannot fight, you can lend your money. Buy bonds or certificates now.' Other banners carried by the cadets carried the warning: 'Starvation stares us in the face unless we economise now' and 'It is what we can do without that counts.'

The procession was met at the entrance to Bedford Circus by the mayor (Mr J. G. Owen), the sheriff (Mr H. C. Rowe), Mr E. S. Plummer (the chairman of the campaign) as well as many other prominent citizens. Among the crowd were a number of wounded soldiers as well as female war workers.

Prior to taking out the first War Bond from the Tank bank, the mayor addressed a few words to the crowd. He reminded his fellow citizens that the time had come for Exeter to make another effort. He went on to say that the city did magnificently in the spring for the Victory War Loan but due to a failure of the Russian Allies on their side, there was still a long way to go before victory was obtained. He continued that although the outlook at the present moment was not what they had hoped, he was sure that the citizens of Exeter, in common with the citizens of the Empire, would not be downhearted but would see it through to the end. He urged them to invest all they could in National War Bonds and said that Exeter had so far contributed £20,000 a week since the beginning of November.

The mayor concluded: 'Some people are saying that the government will repudiate liabilities. So long as the British Empire holds your securities, they will be absolutely safe. That is your security for the money you lend your Government – the British flag – and it rests with us to keep that flag flying in order that our credit may be good and remain good as I'm sure it will.'

The speech was met with much applause.

On 12 December, Mr J. Stocker presided at a meeting of the Exeter Tribunal. There were thirty cases to be heard and most of them were C3 men who were at the tribunal because of their wartime exemption. The chairman stated that the needs of the army were so great that an individual would have to have a very strong case to appeal for exemption. All cases had been put before the tribunal on a previous occasion.

Also on Wednesday 12 December, Mr Horatio Bottomley lectured an audience at Victoria Hall, Exeter, about his experiences during a recent visit to the trenches on the Western Front. His talk was said to be remarkably entertaining and he illuminated his remarks with flashes of humour while also putting across vivid descriptions of the grim tragedies of war. Examples of his humour were reported in the next day's *Western Times*. When asked to wear a lifebelt on the journey over, as it would help keep him afloat, he replied, 'I have done a good deal of floating in my time!' but said the officer didn't appreciate the joke. This banter immensely tickled the audience who had come to hear him speak. He stated, 'There is an old Greek proverb which says that whom the gods love die young. Therefore I shall live to a good old age!'

The article relayed more of Bottomley's quips in which he continued: 'Being no longer in Parliament, I had no difficulty in finding a gas helmet to fit me.' The article continued:

Crossing open country in the firing zone in France, the General told him that in the event of shells dropping, he was to immediately fall down on his stomach.

'I told him,' said Bottomley, 'that if I were to lie down on my stomach in the open country that it would provide the finest possible target for the enemy.' So, he remained on his legs and ultimately reached the trenches. After passing sarcastic references at the Censor, whom he never consulted, he gave thrilling descriptions of the prowess of British airmen at the front and a vivid word-picture of the battlefield of the Somme, where after twelve months, bodies

were constantly being revealed by the action of the weather and burials were still frequent.

During his talk, Bottomley was very optimistic about the war situation. He said that he made no claim to be a military expert but felt that the war would end where it had begun, on the Western Front. 'Give Haig,' he said, 'a free hand without interference from politicians and give him a few weeks' fine weather and he has the enemy in the West absolutely at his mercy.'

He urged the nation to 'stick at it' and felt that the war would soon be over as Germany were on the verge of starvation.

On Thursday 20 December, news was announced of the Exeter War Loan and the recent 'Tank Week'. The *Exeter and Plymouth Gazette* reported:

Mr H Armitage, who, in addition to his duties as clerk to the Exeter Education Committee, has put in many hours as honorary secretary of the War Economy Committee, has prepared some interesting figures in connection with the city's recent Tank week and her total investment in War Loan. So far, as war savings certificates and war bonds are concerned, the amounts invested in Exeter for the three weeks previous to the Tank week were £9,000, £16,000 and £15,000 respectively. The total investment at the Tank, the Banks and the Post Office during Tank week amounted to no less than £42,800, a sum exceeding, of course, the total for the three previous weeks. The Committee are, therefore, entitled to claim that their efforts attained considerable success. This success is, perhaps, more marked when it is realised that before the Tank week was arranged, Exeter had invested £1,250,000 in the various issues of War Loans, £200,000 in war bonds and over £100,000 in war savings certificates, a total of £1,550,000.

The pantomime for Christmas 1917 at the Theatre Royal was *Aladdin*. The *Exeter and Plymouth Gazette* of Saturday 22 December noted:

There are few people at the present time who do not hold the opinion that the innocent fun of pantomime, and like-minded productions, acts as a needed tonic in these times. Visits to places of amusement do not make us forget what the world has at stake but enable us to take our minds off, for a brief spell, the worry and care of daily life. It is pleasing to record, therefore, that the directors of the Theatre Royal, Exeter, have decided to continue the old custom of having a pantomime season this year. The wonderful story of Aladdin and the magic lamp, which is an ever new source of delight to the youngsters, forms the basis of the forthcoming production and no effort has been spared to ensure that the finished article shall be merry and bright.

Theatre Royal, Exeter.

Nightly at 7.15 until further notice.
MATINEES every Tuesday and Friday
at 2 p.m.

EXETER'S 29th GRAND XMAS
PANTOMIME
ALADDIN.

ANOTHER BIG SUCCESS.
Everything to please the Children.
SEATS MAY NOW BE BOOKED.
Box Office, 10.30 a.m. to 10 p.m. Telephone
121

An advert for the Christmas pantomime of 1917. Aladdin *became Exeter's 29th grand Christmas panto and was performed at the Theatre Royal.*

CHAPTER FIVE

1918 – The final blows

In January 1918, sugar was rationed. By the end of April, meat, butter, margarine and cheese were also rationed. Ration cards were issued and people were required to register with their local butcher and grocer. People in Exeter joined long queues to get the basic of foods, including potatoes and many other vegetables.

The *Western Times* of Monday 7 January reported the huge gathering that took place at Exeter Cathedral on the previous day. In response to a call by the king, a service was held of prayer and thanksgiving. It was timed to start at 10am, half-an-hour earlier than usual, so that soldiers could attend. The whole church was filled and there were members of the regular forces, the Depot Devon Regiment from the Higher Barracks and the cadets under training from Topsham Barracks, as well as many wounded troops from the various hospitals around the city. Colonel Koe, who was in command of the 8th Regimental District, and other officers filled the clergy stalls. There were also volunteers and khaki-dressed small boys. Whilst the military element occupied the nave, the seats in front of the pulpit were taken up by municipal representatives. After hymns were sung, prayers were given for anyone closely affected by the war, for the Allies, for allied unity and endurance and for victory and peace.

Similar services were held at non-conformist churches with special prayers said for members of the forces. The services concluded with the National Anthem.

During February, an appeal for a football appeared in the *Western*

A ration book and coupons. Sugar was rationed in January 1918 and by April, meat, butter, margarine and cheese were also rationed. Rationing became a way of life and much was in short supply.

Times from members of the Devonshire Regiment serving in France. A Mr Webber of the Exeter Sports Depot sent one to the mayoress's depot to be forwarded on to the troops. Other donations of footballs were expected and the newspaper commented that 'all would be welcome'. Readers from Plymouth and Exeter were also asked to forward any books and periodicals to the mayoress's depot, which would then be forwarded to the Front.

HMS **Powerful.** *During the First World War, HMS* **Powerful** *and her sister ship, HMS* **Terrible,** *were stripped of their armaments and acted as transport carriers for troops and later served as accommodation vessels.*

On 17 February, the Bishop of Exeter paid a visit to the boys' training establishment at Devonport where he confirmed ninety youths and boys on HMS *Powerful* before holding a service on the *Impregnable*.

Gifts donated to the mayoress's depot included ninety eggs, which were received from the parishes of Chumleigh and Ashreigney, from a Mrs W. P. Martin, together with twenty-four from the children of the

Christow Baptist Sunday School. These were all sent to Nos. 7 and 8 Hospitals in Exeter. Bales of woollens were dispatched to mine-sweepers and fighting units on the Mesopotamia Front, and cases of 'comforts' were sent to Ambulance and Devon units on the Western Front. Cake, which was a gift from a Mr Martin of Chulmleigh, was received for all patients in the military hospital. Altogether, 261 parcels of food and 100 of clothing were sent to prisoners-of-war in German camps. Also sent were international money orders to Turkish and Bulgarian camps and parcels of food through the Central Committee.

On Friday 8 March, an appeal appeared in the *Western Times* requesting 'knitted comforts (socks and scarves), handkerchiefs and bath towelling', which were badly needed by the Devons fighting in Mesopotamia. There was also an appeal for packing paper for the Prisoners-of-War Department and a request asked that any left-over wallpaper from decorating should be handed in to the mayoress's depot.

The *Western Times* of Friday 5 April reported that Second-Lieutenant L. A.W. Vincent, from Exeter, had been missing since 24 March when the German offensive commenced. Second-Lieutenant Vincent was formerly a member of the *Western Times* staff and joined up on the outbreak of war, enlisting with the 11th Hussars. He was transferred to the Yorkshire Regiment with which he went to Gallipoli before serving in Egypt. He was wounded in 1915 while at the Western Front and recommended for a commission in 1917 after passing through the cadet school at Newmarket.

On Saturday 6 April, the *Exeter and Plymouth Gazette* carried a story concerning Exeter's relieving officer who had been forced to join up. The story read:

> *The Exeter panel of the Devon Appeal Tribunal, Sir Ian Amory presiding, was yesterday asked to extend the exemption given to the only male Relieving Officer for Exeter.*
>
> *The Chairman: We think public authorities should set a very bright example. The national need is much greater than it was last October and we are unable to grant the application. The man must serve his country at once. Captain Stirling said the man would get about nine days to comply.*

Zeebrugge sailors on board the **King George V.** *The raid on Zeebrugge on 23 April 1918 by the British Royal Navy effectively put the German naval base at Bruges out of action. The assault was planned and led by Admiral Roger Keyes.*

The *Exeter and Plymouth Gazette* of Friday 26 April carried a story relating to the naval attack on Ostende and Zeebrugge. It read:

> *Exeter has a personal interest in the daring naval attack on Ostende and Zeebrugge, for the commander of one of the old submarines, which were filled with explosives and blown up at the approach to the Mole of Zeebrugge, is Lieut. Sandford, a son of the late Archdeacon of Exeter. In the course of an interview with a Press representative, Lieut. Sandford said that he set the fuse and blew the submarine up at the viaduct and thought things went alright. 'We were lucky in being picked up by the picket-boats afterwards. The firing from the shore was a bit severe at 200 yards and only the fact that the sea was a bit rough, and we were up and down a good deal, saved us.' Devonians in general, and Exonians in particular, will be pleased to hear that the gallant submarine commander returned from his hazardous journey. He is, however, wounded in one of his hands and at present in hospital. Lieut. Sandford has four years'*

experience of submarines in home waters. A Marine officer, writing of the affair, says: 'One of the finest achievements of the undertaking was the dare-devil work of our own submarines. Two of our oldest boats managed to get in under the Viaduct at Zeebrugge and between them, they placed some ten tons of high explosives under the shore end of the Viaduct, which connects the Mole with the shore, blowing it up, and thus completely preventing reinforcements coming from the shore. The force of this explosion made everything rock. It was a daring exploit.'

On 7 May, a boy from Devonport found himself in court after taking an unpaid trip on a train to Exeter. The unnamed boy was described as *'a rosy-faced 11-year-old Devonport lad'*. Chief-Inspector Martin said that the boy was found on the train at St David's Station in Exeter and that he was on his way to see his uncle at Paddington. He gave a false name. When enquiries were made, it was found that the boy's father was in the army and the court was told that he had run away several

Sir Robert Newman pictured with Mrs Oakes, the honorary secretary of the Women's branch of the Exeter Conservative Association, and his agent Mr Andrew.

times before. His mother stated that he had taken money and slept out at night. Apart from that, he was said to be of good character and well behaved at school.

The chairman asked the boy if he would be sorry to be sent to a reformatory, to which he replied, 'I don't mind.'

He added that he wanted to leave home because his sisters told lies about him.

He was fined and ordered to be sent back to Devonport. His mother was left to pay the fare.

On Wednesday 8 May, *The Cornishman* reported that Sir Robert Newman (Conservative) had been returned unopposed for Exeter.

The *Exeter and Plymouth Gazette* of Monday 3 June announced the death of Miss Francis Althea Westron of 3 Elm Grove Road, who was 99. The article described her as having a charming personality and made a delightful companion and 'retained all her faculties to the last'. She was said to be generous and warm-hearted, subscribed to many charities and was the last surviving member of a well-known family in

The mayoress's depot's gifts to prisoners-of-war. The mayoress (Mrs J. G. Owen) and fellow fundraisers are shown outside St Pancras Church.

Somerset. Born in 1819, she had lived through six reigns including George III, George IV, William IV, Victoria, Edward VII and George V. Her memory of past events was said to be remarkable.

On Wednesday 5 June, the *Western Times* published a list of requests from soldiers on the Western Front to the Mayoress of Exeter. These included handkerchiefs (dark shades), towels, anti-vermin vests, cricket sets and footballs.

The *Western Times* of 18 June reported that in the last fortnight, 630 parcels had been dispatched from the Prisoners-of-War Department of the Mayoress of Exeter's Depot to men of the Devon Regiment, who were held prisoner in German camps. One soldier wrote:

> *Your parcel arrived in perfect condition. Everything was much appreciated and we cannot thank you too much for all that you have done for us during our service abroad.*

On 21 June, the Devon Women's War Agricultural Committee met at Exeter and a Miss Calmady-Hamlyn reported on the recent recruitment drive at Plymouth, Exeter and Torquay. She said that the response to their appeal had been most satisfactory, better than in other parts of the country. She stated that at Plymouth seventy new recruits joined up and that the class of recruits was good, not the 'odds-and-ends found in towns'. She was pleased that they consisted of daughters of farmers

The Land Army was set up in Great Britain in 1917. Women played a big role in agricultural work and were asked to sign on for either six months or a year. With many men away fighting, they provided vital service.

and labourers and were generally country girls. Thousands of girls were still needed and it was suggested that they took their recruitment drive to seaside towns during the summer. A Miss Nightingale, for the committee, stated that since the inauguration of the Land Army movement, 337 women had been accepted with 274 working on farms, forty-seven working for the forage department and sixteen working for the timber-cutting section.

Entertainment in the city for the week commencing Monday 15 July was announced in the *Plymouth and Exeter Gazette*. This included Paul Witt and Teddie Butt at the Hippodrome, who were described as 'elite entertainers' and who were making a return to the city by special request. Also on the bill was Haidee Stewart Kingston, described as a refined vocalist, and The Waratahs, direct from Australia. Also listed were Tom Reno (popular comedian), The Brandons (instrumental specialists straight from the London Hippodrome) and Esa Japanese Trio (a balancing act).

Over at the Palladium was *Miss USA* – an exciting story of spies and heroism in five parts starring June Caprice. It was followed later in the week by *What Money Can't Buy*, a drama in four parts starring Jack Pickford and Louise Huff.

At the Empire, in High Street, was the drama *The Hidden Valley*, described as 'the story of a man who risked the unknown and what he found there'. This was followed by *The Danger Signal* (a thrilling drama in five reels).

A group of working lads, mainly messenger boys, gathered for a Sunday evening rally of the YMCA. The photo includes Cadet Lieutenant E. French of the YMCA Terrtorial Cadet Company (Exeter Battalion).

Meanwhile, an illustrated lecture by Captain Alston of the RAF was given at the Barnfield Hall in the presence the mayor, Sir James Owen. Captain Alston was described as a 'fighting pilot from the Western Front' and the show included '100 thrilling lantern slides from the battle area'. Admission was free.

A letter appeared in the *Western Times* of Thursday 25 July under the heading, 'Exeter YMCA Night Patrols.' It read:

Sir, Will you allow me to ask for volunteers for the Exeter YMCA night patrols in the interests of soldiers and sailors coming into our city at night? It is not generally known by the public that service men (frequently on leave from the Front) are continually stranded at the railway stations at night, with no knowledge of the city, and unable to proceed on their journey until the morning trains. We require gentlemen volunteers who will meet the trains both at St David's and at Queen Street and conduct them to the YMCA – which is never shut – and other similar accommodation in the city. The work can be done in three shifts each evening. If sufficient gentlemen will volunteer each to take one of these shifts per week, this work, which is so appreciated by the men, can be easily undertaken.

I am, sir, yours faithfully,
A Rayner-Smith (General Secretary), King's Lodge, Exeter.

On 27 July, the *Western Times* reported the court martial of Devonport Dockyard youths. The article read:

A district court-martial was held at the Town Barracks, Exeter, yesterday for the trial of six conscientious objectors. Major R Coleridge was President and Major Wray was the prosecuting officer.

Private Thomas Wotton, of the Depot Devon Regiment, was charged with disobeying the command of Captain H G Hawker, to put on uniform at Exeter on Monday, 22nd July. It was stated that accused, who had been stationed at the C O camp at Princetown, objected on conscientious grounds to put on the uniform. In a written statement, the accused said he regarded the world as his country, mankind as his brothers, Socialism as his religion and regarded the military system as a menace to human life and to human freedom. A previous conviction of 8 months' imprisonment for a similar offence at Hounslow was recorded.

Ernest G Stowell, aged 19, Gloucester Regiment, attached to the Depot Devon Regiment and formerly employed at Devonport Dockyard, pleaded guilty to a similar offence at the Exeter Town Barracks on July 23rd. Accused, in a written statement, quoted the Scriptures to show that military service was opposed to the will of God. He added that he had no animosity against officers of the British Army but hoped that God might have mercy on them and that they might be saved. He admitted that he was, at the time of being called to the Army, employed in Devonport dockyard but that was the result of circumstances over which he had no control. He explained that he had entered the dockyard at the age of 14, as an apprentice to the electrical engineering, and then had no spiritual experience. At the age of 16, he was converted. He was bound to serve in the dockyard by agreement, to break which would have been a criminal offence. Now, however, that the Government had violated the terms of his indentures by forcing him into the army, he was at liberty to act on his convictions. He objected to military service entirely on religious grounds and not in opposition to the Government of the country. It was recorded that Stowell was at Plymouth fined £2 and ordered to be handed over to the military authorities for being an absentee.

Howard Vincent Evans, aged 19, of the Gloucestershire Regiment, attached to the Depot Devon Regiment, pleaded guilty to a similar offence at Exeter on July 23rd. In a written statement, the accused said that the spirit of the army was out of harmony with the word of Christ. He became an apprentice to the electrical engineering in Devonport dockyard in 1912 but then he was without religious convictions and had no scruples in the matter. In the following year, he underwent a change and since 1916, he had been a worker in the Spiritual field at Plymouth and had acted as a deputy pastor. It was recorded that he had been fined £2 by the Plymouth magistrates for being an absentee and was handed over to the military.

The other three conscientious objectors mentioned in the article had similar religious convictions.

On 16 August, the *Western Times* reported that an Exeter journalist had been wounded while fighting on the Western Front. Corporal Herbert Cater of the Tanks Corps was taken to a Canadian Hospital at Le Trepost, France. His parents, Mr and Mrs J. Cater of Barnstaple, received the news from him in a letter on the previous Tuesday in which he said that he had been hit by shrapnel in the neck but that the wound wasn't serious.

The *Western Times* of 24 August reported about a wounded soldier in hospital in Exeter. The story read:

There is a wounded soldier at No 3 War Hospital, Exeter, who must surely be something of a record holder. He has been fighting continuously for six years and, despite all rough usage to which he has been subjected, seems good for as many more. At the same time, he confesses that he has had enough of war, and little wonder, but there is within him a thirst for vengeance – an undying hate of the Hun.

Michael Vakeleich is a Serbian and just over 27 years ago was born in the city of Preotsky, a town in Central Serbia. At the age of twelve, he left his native country to seek fame and fortune in Canada. He returned home to take up arms in 1914.

His face lights up with enthusiasm as he talks of early battles. Victories over the Turks give him special satisfaction for he detests the Turk. But much as he hates him, his hatred for the man with the fez is as love compared to his hatred for the Germans. When fighting with the Serbians, he was wounded three times and the last injury in his head kept him in hospital for six months. When he had recovered, he was discharged from the Serbian Army and returned to Canada where he received a letter from a cousin who told him that his sister had been shot by the Germans (who were with the Austrians), that they had looted his native town and had hanged his father.

'Then,' he said, 'I hated them more than ever and joined the Canadian Army to get even with them.' He has been wounded twice with the Canadians and has fought with them at Vimy Ridge, Passchendaele, Amiens, the Somme, Arras, Loos and at Roye in the last 'push' when he was wounded.

Vakeleich holds three medals and altogether has been wounded five times (twice in the head, twice in the legs and once in the arm).

He had thirteen relatives fighting, nine of whom have been killed including one brother. One of his brothers is still fighting with the Serbian Army and another is with the Canadians.

Deller Cafe, Exeter. During December of 1916, Messrs Deller's moved from their old premises in ~~hedral~~ *Yard to a new building at the corner of High Street and Bedford Street. A collection box at the café* ~~ed~~ *£5 5s 2d for the Hospitality Fund during the first week of December 1916. Their orchestra played at* ~~London~~ *and South Western Railway Company exhibition of garden produce in August 1918.*

The *Western Times* of Tuesday 27 August published a story about the employees of the London and South Western Railway Company and their contribution to the war effort especially with the production of garden produce to increase the national food supply. Along all parts of the line that had vacant ground, much of it was brought under cultivation by the staff of the railway. Many men also produced food on local allotments. For two years previously, exhibitions of produce, etc, had been held in London but it was decided that such a show would be held in Exeter in 1918 which embraced the line from Salisbury to

Padstow. A committee was set up with Mr A. H. Hoyle, the district superintendent, as president and Mr C. Piper as honorary secretary. The show was held in the Barnfield Hall on Friday 23 August and 190 competitors took part. Prizes were given by the chairman of directors (Brigadier-General Drummond), the directors, Sir Robert Newman MP, the general manager and other chief officers. Mr E. H. Jenkins, FRHS, of London, was the judge. In all cases, competition was keen. Messrs Robert Veitch and Son of Exeter occupied a large stall displaying a fine selection of vegetables and flowers. Under the gallery was a large quantity of garden produce, which was not for the competition but grown for the benefit of the L and S Western Orphanage at Woking, with money raised going to help the organisation.

The show was opened by the deputy mayoress, who remarked that she felt she almost belonged to the L and S W Railway having spent so many hours during the past four years at their station ministering to the soldiers. She took the opportunity to thank the staff for their kind help. The deputy mayoress was presented a bouquet by Miss Peggie Piper, the small daughter of the honorary secretary. A musical programme was provided by Deller's Orchestra, and later in the day a concert was arranged by a Mrs Mairs.

Many prizes were distributed to competitors and the show was hailed a great success.

On 5 September, it was reported that the Bishop of Exeter's third son, Captain John Arthur Cecil, had been killed in action on the Western Front. The Bishop's youngest son, Edward Rupert, had been killed in July 1915 whilst serving with the Bedfordshire Regiment, and his eldest son, Randle William, was killed in December 1917. His second son, Victor Alexander, had been twice wounded while fighting with the Hants Regiment.

On Friday 13 September, the *Western Times* reported the fatality of Rupert James Hill, aged 5, who was the victim of a distressing accident involving a car on the previous Wednesday morning. The boy's father, Lieutenant H. C. Hill, was a member of the Indian Army and was a prisoner-of-war in Turkey. The boy's mother gave evidence at the inquest and stated that they had been in Eland's shop and left to go into Green and Son's when the mother noticed a car approaching. She said to the boy, 'We must mind that car.' She had her hands full of heavy parcels and an umbrella so didn't have hold of the boy. There was a heavy shower at the time and nothing, except for the car, was in the road. They were nearly across the thoroughfare when the boy's mother noticed another car coming the other way. She said to the boy to mind out but he ran forward and the car struck him. A verdict of accidental death was recorded.

On Saturday 14 September, the *Western Times* reported that Mr Bert Vincent of St Thomas, Exeter, had received news that his son, Second Lieutenant Leslie Vincent, had died in the previous March. Mr Vincent had received news that his son was missing but no details were available. However, through the Geneva Red Cross it was learnt that Second Lieutenant Vincent had died in a German Reserve Field Hospital at Cambrai from gunshot wounds on 31 March. Leslie Vincent was only 19 when he joined the forces at the outbreak of war and had previously been an apprentice at the *Western Times* and the *Express and Echo*, where he trained as a printer and linotype operator. He died aged 23. His brother, who was attached to the RAMC, was in hospital in Plymouth, due to illness, after serving four years at the Front.

On Saturday 21 September, a German prisoner-of-war died at No 1

he Eye Infirmary in Exeter in 1914. The infirmary became VA No 1 Hospital, used for the care and eatment of wounded soldiers.

Military Hospital in Exeter. The deceased was a Private Hugo Schrader, aged 29, who was wounded at the Western Front. He was due to be buried at the Higher Cemetery.

Also on Saturday 21 September, the death was reported of Fred Lessons, who was a well-known Southern League player for Northampton. He often played at St James's Park, Exeter, and was very popular with City football followers. He died while fighting at the Front.

The *Western Times* of Monday 30 September reported on Exonians boxing at the front. The article read:

> *The way they do it in Canada is to arrange a concert party, interspersed with boxing bouts and the joint affair goes off champion.' Thus writes an Exonian from the Western Front who has recently taken part in such an event out there. In a six-round contest Spr. Davey, Devon Fortress R.E. (Exeter) beat Pte. MacGauley, 24th Field Ambulance (Exeter) after a good show in the fifth round, the R.E. being stronger and heavier. The star turn was a 10-round contest between Pte. Holland (Canada) and Pte. Tom Tootell, 24th Field Ambulance (Exeter). Holland was the runner-up for the championship recently held in France, whilst Tootell will be remembered in Exeter as a 'bit of a bloke' before emigrating to Canada two years before the war. Tootell was the victor on this occasion, knocking out his opponent in the fourth round. The correspondent concludes: 'The noble art, like everything else with us, is going strong and we are now anticipating a meeting between Tootell and J. Driscoll (gymnasium instructor).*

Mrs Prescott of Exeter received a letter from the chaplain informing her of the death in action of her husband, Sergeant J. H. Prescott, on 7 October. The letter said that they were returning from the line after a very successful advance when a shell burst right in the middle of the party. Sergeant Prescott was killed instantly. The chaplain added, 'He was such a fine soldier, so capable and dependable, and his loss is indeed a very sad one.'

Before the war, Sergeant Prescott was an instructor at the Higher Barracks where, it was said, he was much beloved by all those who came into contact with him.

e Theatre Royal in Exeter. Entertainment carried on throughout the war and showed some major oductions, including the annual pantomime.

On Wednesday 9 October, General Biddle, the commander of the American Forces in England, addressed a crowded audience at the Theatre Royal, Exeter. He stated that having come into the war, President Wilson was determined that the enemy should regret it and regret it deeply. General Biddle received a friendly welcome and said that the aim of his visits was so that the people of Britain and America could understand one another better. He continued that all parts of Great Britain had received American troops with great hospitality and wished to express his gratitude whilst in Exeter.

'We are now in the fight,' he went on, 'and we can be forgiven when we say that America is proud of her fighting sons (cheers). They have already shown the highest qualities as soldiers and, in that section of the Western Front where I have been, they have owed much of their success to the brilliant example of the French and British. In some of our divisions in France, as many as twelve to fifteen languages are spoken but it makes no difference from what parts the American Army come: they are all alike, determined to fight on – fight bravely to the very end.'

The speech was met with much applause.

On the Saturday evening of 12 October, a large crowd assembled in Bedford Circus to witness a series of war films under the auspices of the Ministry of National Service. The chairman of the evening was the deputy mayor (Mr T. Bradley Rowe). A photograph of David Lloyd George and his achievements formed a conspicuous feature of the programme. The cinema was on tour in the west of England under the management of Stephen Scott and a Mr Hutson. The pictures shown on the screen were divided into three sections; 'Sons of the Sea', 'Women and the War' and 'The Western Front'.

On Tuesday 12 November 1918, the *Western Morning News* carried the headline, '*CRUSHING ARMISTICE TERMS'*. The article stated:

The last shot, it is to be presumed and hoped, has been fired in the greatest war ever known.

At 5 o'clock yesterday morning the armistice was signed by the plenipotentiaries and came into operation six hours later (11 a.m.).'

The crowd at Buckingham Palace on Armistice Day. Thousands of cheering spectators lined streets to celebrate the end of the war.

On Tuesday 12 November, the *Western Times* published a story under the headline 'The Enthusiasm of a Great Crowd: Tears of Joy.' The article read:

The news was posted in the window of the Western Times office at exactly twelve minutes to eleven and High Street became immediately transformed into a jubilant, cheering mass of citizens of all ages, all conditions.

It was the long expected news at last! All day Sunday people had remained in the principal thoroughfare, anxiously awaiting its arrival, and for hours Sunday night, there were thousands massed between Bedford Circus and Queen Street on the tip-toe of expectancy. It was not until 10 o'clock Sunday evening that they began to thin and not until eleven that the street resumed its normal night appearance.

At 10 am yesterday, there was just the ordinary traffic in the High Street – nothing more. Pedestrians went stolidly about their usual business, and though there was a lively sense of the nearness of great events in the minds of everyone, it was well concealed.

Just after ten, the first heralding of the news came along. The phone wires at the W.T. office bore the information that Plymouth had picked up an Admiralty wireless to the affect that the armistice had been signed, and that flags were flying in the town and bands blaring forth the good tidings. Then a ring from Torquay! The same news there. Listen at the phone receiver! One could hear the bands playing and the wild exultant shouting of the people in the Torquay main street.

Ten minutes later and a hurried message came to hand from the Exeter Post Office. The news at last! Official, this time, without a doubt – without a shadow of doubt! The fateful epoch-making document signed at 5am and fighting to stop at 11am – fighting to stop after these four years of agony!

At twelve to eleven, the announcement was posted in the Western Times window and at once began this remarkable transformation of which we have spoken. A cheer! And another and another. 'Thank God! Hurrah! Hurrah!' A running and clattering of feet. The news being shouted up and down the city and then people hurrying from everywhere. They came in hundreds. Boys and children scampered waving flags and shouting; clerks left their stools and hurried out hatless; young lady shop assistants, hatless too, came pell-mell scurrying to the scene; the swelling crowd pressed to within view of the posted announcement and soon the street was a swaying mass of jubilant, cheering, hat and flag waving rejoicers.

It was an unforgettable scene as the news spread and spread and perhaps the phase of it which will leave the deepest impression on one's mind was a picture of weeping women. They passed along – there were quite a number of them – with tears of sheer joy coursing down their cheeks, what time the youngsters were shouting themselves hoarse. The flags had already appeared at the Guildhall waving triumphantly in the fresh morning breeze; each window soon bore its Union Jack and across the main street fluttered a bold line of our national emblems, overlooking the joy of the surging crowd, as it stretched down the thoroughfares, its pent-up feelings at last finding vent and play.

One big Colonial corporal careered along dancing and every now and again stopping to shake hands with friend and with stranger, kissing the girls and lifting aloft the kiddies. Wounded soldiers in their hospital blue went along arm in arm ringing a school bell, twirling a hand rattle, their adventures of the battle-field forgotten for the nonce. A procession of young women and lad munition workers strode to the scene in their overalls, cheering and singing, and a group of Colonial soldiers had already set the bell a-ringing at St Petrock's, stopping only when people began to troop inside, thinking that the first of the thanksgiving services was already being commenced.

As mid-day neared, the crowds became more and more dense. The whole of High Street was a slowly moving, parading throng. Two wounded Australian privates outside the Guildhall, in the midst of their strident cheering, turned suddenly and grasped the hand of a British captain in a shake of joy; the next moment the three of them were there dancing a can-can of delight. Everybody and his neighbour, as the saying goes, had left work and trooped into the streets and elderly citizens and usually very staid and phlegmatic citizens were in the very centre of the rejoicings, taking a foremost share in them. Some of Hele's schoolboys, fifty or more, came marching along in procession, adding their treble, high-pitched notes to the volume of triumphant choruses; a few convalescents from the military hospitals, not stopping even to put on coats, had run to join the crowds in their shirt-sleeves.

Among them was a Canadian and it was fitting that just as he passed along, the notice should be posted in the Western Times window:

'At dawn today the Canadians captured Mons.' Mons! What memories the name recalled.

The youngsters in the streets were by this time sharing in a

Armistice celebrations with many happy faces and much flag waving. American flags were waved alongside British ones and everyone was jubilant that the war was finally over.

gratuitous supply of cocked-hats made from a series of paper Union Jacks by the staff of Messrs. Walton and Co., and given away, as they were quickly given out, by the proprietor.

At noon, Old Glory, with its Stars and its Stripes, was unfurled from the Guildhall and very soon, on either side of it, flew brave Belgium's colours and the Tricolour of France, avenged. High over the three, ran still the Union Jack and below, in the street, passing backwards and forward in front of the old, grey front of the Guildhall, the flags and the badges and the emblems of red, white and blue increased in dozens, in hundreds. Up the Fore Street hill, drawn by an old farm pony, came a little four-wheeler carrying a quartet of bedecked girl land-workers; they were dressed in their brown, field garb; they too had 'downed tools' and hurried into the city to share in the excitement.

Long before one o'clock, the great majority of business establishments closed down for the day and all classes of people gave themselves over to the sweeping wave of sheer joy that had surged through the city. Impromptu processions still filed up and down High Street, St Sidwell's and Fore Street and it was wonderful how many thousands of flags had come suddenly to light. The whole city was ablaze with them – simply ablaze, and by this time the posters had already announced the afternoon Cathedral service and services at many other places of worship in the city. As one read these announcements, one gave a thought – a deep thought – to the dead, the great dead, who have made the Supreme Sacrifice for this Supreme Victory of Right, the Immortal Dead. In an hour like this, their memory is a thousand-fold precious, a thousand-fold revered.

Between one and two o'clock, confetti made its appearance in the streets and soon the roadways were smothered with it. The trams – all the trams which passed – were crowded and from them all streamed flags and favours. At the rear of one, as it went along St Sidwell's, fluttered a Belgian flag, bright and new, its yellow band flashing as the car sped its way; a Belgian refugee walking on the pathway gave way to his feelings as he caught sight of it and, running up to the back of the car, raced beside it and, taking the flag from the hand which held it, waved it excitedly over his head; then passed it back to its owner and resumed his journey, flushed and panting.

Whistles, toy-trumpets and bugles were everywhere and always up and down the main street, up and down its full length, the people (all workers out to air their joy) passed slowly to the waving of a myriad of Union Jacks. A procession of schoolboys from mean streets threaded the path through the throng; people stood aside for them to go, for their approach was heralded by the beating of their improvised drums; one drum was an old kettle and another a bucket, upon which a stocky youngster, shoulders thrown back, was beating his martial rat-a-tat-tat in quite a good imitation of the music of the throbbing kettle-drum.

On the top of one car were twenty or so Colonials and wounded Britishers, their tunics and hats afire with the Red, White and Blue as they sang and laughed and cheered. So, as the afternoon wore on, Exeter settled down to its Armistice Day gaiety, each hour

The Mayor of Exeter (Sir James Owen) addressing the Armistice Day crowd at the Buller Statue, which was published in the Western Times *of Friday 15 November 1918.*

bringing its new diversion and adding to the multitude of flags fluttering, waving and dancing everywhere.

On Friday 15 November, the *Western Times* published a photo showing a huge gathering at the Buller statue, which showed the mayor addressing the crowd on Armistice Day.

The war had been a long and bloody one. Exeter had played a major part in the struggle. With the war over there wasn't a family there who hadn't lost a son, father, nephew, uncle or brother. There were tremendous celebrations in the streets as the end of the war was announced but the effects of the conflict lasted for years to come.

Bibliography

Newspapers

The Derby Daily Telegraph

The Devon and Exeter Gazette

The Evening Herald

The Exeter and Plymouth Gazette

The Flying Post

The Lady's Pictorial

The North Devon Journal

The Taunton Courier and Western Advertiser

The Western Morning News

The Western Times

The Yellowstone News

Websites

Exeter Memories at www.exetermemories.co.uk/

Index

Adams, Pte F., 85
Aeolian Hall, London, 96
Aerial Danes, 83
Ainsworth, Miss Gladys, 56
Airship, 50
Airy, Rev'd W.S., 56
Aladdin, 115–16
Albion Place, 68
Alexandra Day Committee, 69
Alexandria, 66
Alford, Martin, 71
Alford, Walter, 39
Allies, 7, 59, 77, 113, 117
Allotments, 97–8, 129
Almy, Mr, 89–91
Alston, Capt, 126
America, 47, 98, 133
Amiens, 128
Anciffe's *Nights of Gladness,* 58
Andrew, Miss, 20–1
Andrew, Mr, 122
Anger, Pte P., 85
Anstey, Maj Alfred, 26
Anthrax, 59–60
Anzac Day, 99
APC Section, 63
Aplin, Sergeant, 54, 99
Arbuthnot, Rear Adml, 81
Archdeacon of Exeter, 121
Armistice, 134–5, 137, 139–40
Armitage, Mr H., 115
Army discharge certificate, 82

Army Pay Department, 100, 102,
    104
Army Reserve, 9
Arras, Battle of, 113, 128
Arundel, Maj, 60
Ashreigney, 119
A Tight Corner, 105
Attwood, Horace, 39
Australia, 125
Australian, 33, 99–101, 136
Australian Soldiers' Societies, 99
Austria, 7, 128
Austria-Hungary, 7

Babes in the Wood, 72
Baker, Leonard Philip, 88
Balkwill, William Henry, 95
Ball, J., 84
Baltic Exchange, 7
Bamforth, Miss, 77
Bangalore, 62
Barley, 97
Barnes, Edward, 104
Barnes, Florence Mabel, 104
Barnes, Hilda Jane Millicent, 104
Barnes, Q.M.S., 67–8
Barnes, Sgt Frank, 67–9
Barnfield, 96
Barnfield Hall, 126, 130
Barnstable, 9, 53
Basey, Sgt, 84

Baten, S.B., 84
Battalion of the Royal Defence
  Corps, 82
Bay of Biscay, 48
Bedford Circus, 53, 112–13, 134–5
Bedford Street, 92, 113, 129
Beer, 84
Belgians, 19–20, 40
Belgium, 8, 16, 37, 54, 59, 138
Bengey, Pte H.E., 88
Bere Ferrers Station, 87
Berlin, 90–1, 106
Betty, 109
Bickle, Pte E., 88
Biddell, Maj, 17
Biddle, Gen, 133
Biffen, Mr, 64
Bioscope, 107
Birch, Mr E., 80
Birkett, Capt, 17
Bishop of Exeter, 112, 119, 130
Bishop's Palace, 27
Blackall Road, 29
Black Bull Road, 112
Blackmore, PC, 82
Black Prince, The, 81
Blanchard, A., 84
Blighty, 87
Board of Education, 104
Boche, 83
Boer War, 9, 28
Bonaparte, Prince Victor, 59
Bonhay Road, 11
Borderers, The, 67
Bottomley, Mr Horatio, 114–15
Boundy, Mr G.L., 38
Bovey Tracey, 84
Bowden, A., 84
Bowerman MP, Mr, 71
Bowhay Nurseries, 74
Boxing Day, 43

Boy Scouts, 56
Bradford, Dr, 24
Bradford, Pte E., 42
Bradninch, 27, 85
Bradshaw's Railway Guide, 103
Brandons, The, 125
Bridge Street, 95, 97
Bridgwater, 56–7
Bridle, Pte Frederick William, 28
Brie, 96
Bristol, 56–7
Britannia, 9, 77
British Empire, 7, 113
British Expeditionary Force, 16, 25
British Fleet, 78
British Red Cross Society, 69
Brittain, John, 107
Brock, Capt W., 17, 66
Brock, Councillor W., 10
Brooks, G., 84
Bruges, 121
Buckingham Palace, 12, 134
Bugle Band, The, 98
Bulford, 51
Buller, Miss, 105
Buller's Own, 69
Buller Statue, 139–40
Burgess, Pte J., 88
Burmah, 59
Burridge, Sgt C., 88
Burvill, Gunner Fred, 112
Burvill, Sgt H.A., 112
Butler, Miss Molly, 94
Butt, Teddie, 125
Bystock, 74

C2, 89
C3, 114
Cadet Brigade, 84
Calmady-Hamlyn, Miss, 124
Cambrai, 131

Camden, Spr F., 77
Canadians, 33, 128–9, 137
Canterbury, 51
Capper, Mr Alfred, 95–6
Caprice, June, 125
Cardiff, 13
Carter, Mr C.H., 93
Carter, Mr G.S.B., 92–3
Carter, Mrs W.E., 92
Caruso, 94
Cary Arms, 90
Castle Yard, 17
Cater, Corporal Herbert, 128
Caterpillar Tractors, 87
Cathedral School Cadet Company,
    85
Cathedral Yard, 129
C Company 4th Battalion Highland
    Light Infantry, 53
Cecil, Capt John Arthur, 130
Cecil, Edward Rupert, 130
Cecil, Lord William, 112
Cecil, Lt Randle William, 112
Cecil, Victor Alexander, 130
Central Association Volunteer
    Training Corps, 52–3
Central Powers, 7
Central Serbia, 128
Challice, Mr, 51–2
Chambers, 2nd Lt A.J.F., 77
Chatworthy, Spr E., 77
Chenneour, Pte Edwin G., 59
Cheriton Fitzpaine, 39
Chimes, The, 58
Chittlehampton, 87
Christmas, 38, 41, 43, 45, 47, 49,
    51, 72, 90, 92, 94, 115–16
Christow Baptist Sunday School,
    120
Chumleigh, 119
Church Army Huts, 95–6

Church Road, 20
Churston, 8
Cinderella, 93–4
Cinematograph, 81
City Collar Works, 48–9
City Council, 51, 75, 97, 103
City of Exeter Regiment, the
    Athletes' Volunteer Force, 57
City Hospital at Heavitree, 27, 111
Clark, Lt-Col S.F., 26
Clay, James, 71
Clayton, Capt A.E., 105
Clementine, Princess, 59
Clift, Spr Harry, 28
Cobley, Pte N.J., 88
Coldstream Guards, 28, 37
Cole, Lt P.J., 87
Coleridge, Maj R., 126
Coles, F.F., 89
Coles, Spr A., 77
College Hostel at Bradninch House,
    27
Colleton Crescent, 86
Combemartin, 84
Commercial Road, 97
Compulsory enlistment, 16, 73
Conscientious objectors, 73, 126–7
Coombe Pyne, 84
Coombe Street, 21, 88
Cooper, George, 95
Cosham, F., 103
Cottage Hostel, 98
Couldridge, Miss Rosa, 74
County Ground, 20, 53
Cowick Street, 59
Cowie, Stanley, 34, 36
Cowley Bridge, 95, 105
Cowley Bridge Road, 95
Crawley, Mr, 61
Crediton, 74, 85
Crees, Mrs W., 56

Crete, 59
Crocker, Pte C., 26
Crowdy, Dr F., 59
Cudmore, Pte Albert Henry, 62
Cudmore, Pte George, 62
Cullompton, 36
Cullwick, J., 84
Cumming, Alderman, 90
Cyclist Company South Midland
    Mounted Division, 56
Cyprus Terrace, 62
Czar, 82

Dagsworthy, Mr W.A., 55
Dandini, 94
Danger Signal, The, 125
Daniel, E.R., 89
D'Arcy, Sgt, 78
Dartmouth, 16, 85, 94
Davey, Dr Henry, 65
Davey, Spr, 132
Daw, Joshua, 64
Dawlish, 84
Day, L-Cpl W.R., 88
DCLI, 28, 50
DCM, 78
Defence, The, 81
Della Cassa Sisters, 83
Deller's Café, 92
Deller's Orchestra, 130
Depot Somerset LI, 105
Derby, Lord, 71
Deserter, 94
Despatches, 51
Deutsche Luftschiffahrts-AG
    (DELAG), 52
Devon and Cornwall Branch of the
    National Poor Law Officers'
    Association, 80
Devon and Somerset Stores, 54, 68
Devon Fortress, 132

Devonport, 59, 66, 80, 119, 122–3,
    126–7
Devonport Dockyard, 66, 126–7
Devon Reserves, 10–11, 13
Devons, 8–9, 15, 21, 25–6, 38, 41–
    2, 54, 59–60, 62, 67–9, 71, 73,
    83, 86, 88, 120
Devons and Dorsets, 83
Devonshire Regiment, 13, 28, 53,
    58, 62, 68–9, 119
Devon Terriers, 24
Devon Voluntary Aid Organization,
    24
Devon Women's War Agricultural
    Committee, 124
De Vries, M. Henri, 81
Dimond, L-Cpl, 85
Director-General of Voluntary
    Organizations, 101, 107
Doidge, E.F., 89
Domestic Bazaar Company, 23
Dragoon Guards, 16, 29
Drake, Francis H.L., 90–1
Drake, G.A., 97
Drew, Capt, 17
Driscoll, J., 132
Driver, A.H., 84
Drummond, Brig-Gen, 130
Dublin, 78
Duke of Cornwall's Light Infantry,
    50
Dunsford, Percy, 72
Durham, 84
DVAO, 44
Dyer, Sgt, 24–5

Eastgate, 11
Edward VII, 124
Edwards, Detective, 104
Efford Cemetery, 87
Egypt, 28, 59, 106, 120

Elementary Education Sub-
Committee, 53
Elephant Inn, 109
Elliott, Francis, 89
Elm Grove Road, 123
Elmside, 34
Empire, 7, 39, 86, 91, 113
Empire Pageant, 77
Empire, The, 86–7, 125
England, A., 84
Equipment Fund, 85
Esa Japanese Trio, 125
Esplanade, 56
Evans, Howard Vincent, 127
*Every girl has a Tommy
somewhere,* 94
Exemption, 78, 89–91, 114, 120
Exeter Athletic Volunteer Corps, 31
Exeter Automobile Association, 55
Exeter Battalion Devonshire
Volunteer Regiment, 95
Exeter Cadet Battalion, 85
Exeter Cathedral, 36, 87, 117
Exeter Cathedral School Cadet
Corps, The, 36
Exeter cattle market, 14
Exeter Central, 87
Exeter City, 23, 34, 36–8, 48
Exeter City Workhouse, 80
Exeter Conservative Association,
50, 122
Exeter Convent, The, 40
Exeter Cycling Club, 58
Exeter FC Reserves, 41
Exeter Hut, 110
Exeter Juvenile Court, 102
Exeter Male Voice Choir, 17
Exeter National Relief Fund (Prince
of Wales's appeal), 16
Exeter's Own, 35, 39–40
Exeter Sports Depot, 119

Exeter Swimming Baths, 53
Exeter Theatre, 25, 42, 54
Exeter Tribunal, 78, 88, 114
Exeter University College
Contingent of the 4th Devon
Territorials, 33
Exeter War Relief Committee, 16
Exeter War Savings, 112
Exmouth, 74, 78, 85, 113
Expeditionary Force, 16, 25, 35, 51,
87
Exwick Mills, 7
Eynon, R.H., 84

Fairfield, 32
Fairlie, Miss Winifred, 94
Farthing Breakfast Fund, 97
Father Christmas, 72
Fenwick, G., 56
Fenwick, J., 56
Ferdinand, Franz, 7
Festubert, 38, 41
Fewins, PC W.T., 104
Field Ambulance, 14–15, 45, 49,
132
Fife and Drum Band, 98, 113
Flanders, 110
Folkestone, 111
Food Prices, 17–18
Football, 14, 19, 21–3, 28, 34–8,
48–9, 67, 117, 119, 124, 132
Footballers' Battalion, 49
Ford, Pte A., 85
Ford, Pte J., 84
Fore Street, 10, 32, 138
Forget-Me-Not Day, 63, 101
Formby, George, 94
Fortescue, Earl, 71
France, 16, 25, 59–60, 73, 106,
110–11, 114, 119, 128, 132–3,
138

French, Cad Lt E., 125
French, Field Marshal Sir John, 25
French, General, 51
French Republic, 7
Fred Powell and Co, 107
Friars, The, 98–9
Friary Lane Station, 87
Frog Street, 95
Furber Ambulances, 73
Fusiliers, The, 66

Gabriel, Joseph D., 107
Gaitch, J., 56
Gallipoli, 66, 99, 106, 120
Gas, 51–2, 78, 114
Gater, Miss, 63
Geneva Red Cross, 131
George III, 124
George IV, 124
George V, 66, 121, 124
German prisoners, 16
German Reserve Field Hospital, 131
Germany, 7–9, 23, 52, 98, 115
Getting the dinner in, 107
Gibbings, A., 56
Gibraltar, 55
Gilbert, Yvette, 94
Gill, Lt W.T., 29
Girl From Kays, The, 25
Girl in the Taxi, The, 58
Glanfield, T., 84
Glanville, G., 84
Gloucester, 56
Gloucester Regiment, 127
Gloucesters, The, 57
Glynn, Miss, 43
Goddwin, F., 48
Godfrey, Pte Charles, 53
God Save the King, 30
Gordon Highlanders, 71

Gordon Lamp, 55
Gosport, 48
Gould, Joseph, 79, 86
Gould, Lt Ernest, 87
Graeme, Col, 53
Grant, Pte R., 85
Graslawn, 95
Great Adventure, The, 31
Green, A.T., 34, 36, 48
Green and Son, 130
Greenaway, Sid, 34, 36, 48
Guildford-Quin, Miss Eva, 33
Guildhall, 16, 23, 25, 32, 38–40, 52, 59, 74, 99, 108, 136, 138

Hall, H.L., 56
Hancock, Lt R.E., 34
Hancock, Sgt, 77
Hants Regiment, 130
Hardy-Harris, Mr and Mrs G., 108
Harland, Robert, 94
Hartland, 84
Hawker, Capt H.G., 126
Hawkes, Bugle-Maj, 98–9
Heanton Punchardon, 84
Hearne, Nan C., 107
Heavitree, 27, 34, 55, 110–11
Hedger, Cpl L., 85
Hele, 99, 109, 136
Hidden Valley, The, 125
Higher Barracks, 11, 13, 17, 117, 132
Higher Cemetery, 109, 132
Higher Market, 13
Highland Light Infantry, 32, 53
High Street, 9, 21, 32, 54, 99, 112–13, 125, 129, 135–6, 138
Hill, Lt H.C., 130
Hill, Mr, 103
Hill, Rupert James, 130
Hill, Sgt Norman, 37

Hill, Pte T., 85
Hillman, Pte H., 85
Hinton Lake and Son, Messrs J., 21
Hippodrome, The, 75, 105–107, 125
Hobbs, J., 56
Holland, Pte., 132
Holloway Street, 99
Home Service Garrison Battalion, 81
Honey, A.L., 89
Honeybun, Trooper J., 88
Honiton, 74
Hood, R/Adml, 81
Hood, Sgt-Maj T., 40
Hopping, Miss, 53
Horrabridge, 66
Hospitality Fund, 21, 38, 60, 62–3, 67, 101, 129
Hounslow, 127
Hoyle, Mr A.H., 130
Hoyles, Mr W.E., 74
HRH The Prince of Wales, 12
Huff, Louise, 125
Huns, The, 40, 84, 112
Hurford, Pte R.C., 85
Hutson, Mr, 134
Huxtable, Pte, 85

Ide, 84
India, 33–4, 40, 48, 56, 59, 130
Indefatigable, The, 81
Infantry Record Office, 67–8
Influenza, 51
Invincible, The, 81
Isaacs, Driver W., 88
Italy, 60

Jackman, Percy, 28
James, Mr Frederic, 17
James, Second-Cpl, 77

Janson, Mrs and Miss, 38
Jenkins, Mr E.H., 130
Jenkins, Pte, 85
Jerrett, C.J., 84
Johnstone, Pipe-Maj, 17
Jutland, 79, 81

Kelland, P., 102
Kellet, Mr Arthur, 17
Kendall, Maj, 90
Kerswell, Mr G., 33, 74
Kiff, B., 84
Kilgannon, Drummer, 28
Kinaham, Pte James, 38
King and Queen, The, 64–6, 86
King, Mr W. Kendall, 12, 16, 23, 79
King's Hall, The, 33
King's Liverpool Regiment, 83
King's Lodge, 126
King's shilling, 39
Kingston, Haidee Stewart, 125
Kingsway Theatre, London, 33
Kitchener, 46
Kitchener's Army, 13–14, 17, 20, 25
Kitson, J., 84
Knight, Lt, 113
Knowles, Pte C., 85
Koe, Col, 117

Land Army, 124–5
L and S Western Orphanage, 130
Langdon Thomas, Capt, 56
Langford, Canon and Mrs, 62
Lauder, Harry, 94
Launceston, 50
Lear, Driver W., 88
Lee, Pte W., 66
Legion of Honour, 29
Le Marseillaise, 30

Leopold of Belgium, King, 59
Lessons, Fred, 132
Le Trepost, 128
Levett, Pte C., 85
Lewis, Larry, 107
Liege Horticulture College, 54
Lifton, 84
Lighting, 50, 75, 87, 89, 94, 102
Lighting Committee, 75
Linen League, 23–4
Lion, HMS, 43
Lloyd George, David, 134
London, 7, 19–20, 27, 33, 49, 61,
    87, 90, 94, 96–7, 100, 104, 109,
    125, 129–30
London and South Western
    Railway, 104, 129
London Hippodrome, 125
London Inn Square, 11
London's Playhouse Theatre, 27
London Waterloo, 87
Longbrook Street, 57
Loos, 68–9, 128
Louville, Mr Arthur, 94
Lyme Regis, 56

MacGauley, Pte, 132
Maddock, L-Cpl J.S., 88
Madge, Pte A., 85
Madge, Pte L., 85
Magdalen Street, 78
Mairs, Mrs, 130
Mallett, Mr W.R., 7
Manor Hall, 56
Marlborough House, 96
Martin, Inspector, 22, 82
Martin, Mr, 120
Martin, Mrs W.P., 119
Martin's Lane, 50
Mary Goes First, 27
Mary, Queen, 65–6

Max joins the Colours, 81
Mayoress of Exeter, 20, 23–4, 38,
    41–2, 58, 60–3, 66, 77, 91, 101,
    124
Mayor of Exeter, 12, 31, 39, 52, 71,
    79, 101, 139
McLaren, Canon, 100
McLaren, Elsie, 101
Medical Board, 90
Medland, C.F., 84
Melhuish, Pte G., 85
Melville, 109
Merwin, Bannister, 81
Mesopotamia, 120
Mesopotamia Day, 98
Milford Haven, 15
Military Medal, 109–10
Millbay, 9
Milton Brothers, The, 107
Minhenick, W., 84
Ministry of National Service, 134
Mint School, 32
Miss USA, 125
Modern School at Bishop Blackall,
    27
Mons, 16, 47, 51, 68, 137
Montana, 98
Moon-struck, 56
Moore, Mr F.T., 78–9
Morchard Bishop, 84
Morgan, Mr and Mrs H.G., 75
Mother Goose, 42–3
Motor ambulance, 44
Motorcycle Army Unit Battalion,
    16
Moulding, Mr T., 52
Mount Bath Road, 11
Mount Pleasant Road, 24
Municipal Officers, 73
Munro, Mr, 10
Munro, Mr H.J., 103

Napoleon, Princess Victor, 59
National Anthem, 9, 75, 117
National Reserve, 10, 17,
Nevasa, HM Transport, 24
New Army, 13–14, 20
Newcombe, F., 56
Newman, Sir Robert, 50, 122–3, 130
Newmarket, 120
Newport, 110–11
Newport Hut, 110
Newton Poppleford, 42
Newton, Scout Patrol Ldr William H., 42
Newton VAO, 108
New Zealand, 91, 99
New Zealand Expeditionary Force, 87
Nicholson, A.F., 103
Nicks, Pte E., 85
Nightingale, Miss, 125
Non-conformist, 117
Northampton, 132
North Devon Hussars, 87
Northernhay, 17, 58, 68–9
North Road Station, 66
North Street, 113
Notley, Pte F., 85
Nottingham, 71
Nurses, 31, 55, 60, 65, 70, 111

Oakes, Mrs, 122
Old Glory, 138
Old Tiverton Road, 11, 105
Oliver, Miss, 87
Oliver, Mr A.T., 87
Oliver, Mrs W.H., 87
Osmond, Flying Lt Edward, 47
Osmond, Reginald Charles, 82
Ostende, 121

Owen, James G., 52, 74–5, 78, 88, 113, 126, 139
Owen, James G., Mrs, 108, 123
Oxford, 109

Padstow, 130
Passchendaele, 128
Paignton, 59
Paine, Frank, 91
Palladium, 81, 86–7, 125
Palmer, Bandmaster, 113
Palmer, Lt. A.R., 98–9
Pals battalions, 46
Pantomime, 42–3, 45, 72, 93–4, 115–16, 133
Park Road, 39
Paris, 7
Paris Street, 42, 81
Passmore, Miss Gertrude Isabella, 62
Paste, 81
Pathe Gazette, 81
Payne, J.E., 71
Pennsylvania Temporary Hospital, 51
Pensford, Pte E., 88
Perham Down, 30
Perriam, Mr J., 59
Perriam, Pte Albert, 59
Pickard, Lt-Col R., 45
Pickford, Jack, 125
Pinhoe, 56
Pinhoe Road, 82
Piper, Mr C., 130
Piper, Miss Peggie, 130
Plymouth, 9, 13, 24–5, 33, 41–2, 47, 49, 53, 66, 80, 82, 84–5, 87, 98, 109, 119, 124, 127, 131, 135
Plymsell, Pte F., 85
Plumber, Mr E., 35
Plummer, Mr E.S., 74, 86, 111, 113

Police Force, 9–10, 25
Polsloe Road, 92
Portland Street, 28
Port View, 109
Post Office, 28, 110, 115, 135
Potash and Perlmutter, 109
Powderham Crescent, 87
Powerful, HMS, 119
Preotsky, 128
Prescott, Mrs, 132
Prescott, Sgt J.H., 132
Prince of Wales National Relief
    Fund, 12
Princetown, 126
Pring, Alderman T.C., 38
Prisoners of war, 67, 120, 123–4
Procter, Pte Arthur Henry Herbert,
    83
Prowse, Spr R., 88
Pullen, Dr Bingley, 55–6
Pullen, Miss J., 56

Quance, R., 84
Queen Mary, The, 81
Queen's Theatre, London, 109
Queen Street, 99, 126, 135
Queen Street Station, 15, 38, 68

Rabjohns, Pte, 49
Rack Street, 21
Radcliffe, Spr Ernest Francis, 110
Radley, Corporal E., 35
Railways, 11
RAMC, 35, 109–10, 131
RAMC (Wessex Field Ambulance),
    14–15
Ration cards, 117
Ray, Pte David, 53
Rayner-Smith, A., 126
Ready for Reno, 81
Red Cross flags, 69

Reed, Arthur C., 86
Reed, Rev'd Clifford, 110
Reed, W.H., 110
Registration card, 82, 94
Regulation of Forces act, 1871, 11
Relieving Officer, 120
Rendle, Bandsman VC, DCLI, 50
Reno, Tom, 125
Reuter, 7
Reynolds, Pte F., 85
Richards, Col, 74, 95
Ridge, W., 84
River Exe, 88
RNVR, 89, 90
Roach, Private A., 38
Roberts, Catherine, 100, 102, 104
Roberts, Lord, 22
Roberts, Percy, 100, 102, 104
Roberts, Pte S., 88
Robert Veitch and Son, Messrs, 130
Rockwood Red Cross Hospital, 59
Rodgman, Flt-Sgt Arthur G., 109
Romaine, Claire, 54
Rose Day, 69
Rosevear, Miss Dorothy, 94
Ross, Charles J., 86, 89, 92
Roto-o-rangi, 91
Rousham, Special Constable, 84
Rowe, Bradley, 99, 134
Rowe, H.C., 111, 113
Royal Canadian Regiment , 109
Royal Circus and Menagerie, 82
Royal Devon Yeomanry Cavalry, 11
Royal Field Artillery, 9, 25
Royal First Devon Yeomanry, 28
Royal Flying Corps, 109
Royal Irish Rifles, 78
Royal Mail, 92
Roye, 128
Rule Britannia, 9, 77
Russia, 7, 113

Russian Cossacks, 82
Russian Empire, 7

St David's, 8, 31, 53, 122, 126
St James' Girls School, 77
St James' Park, 23, 95
St John's Hospital School, 83
St Julien, 110
St Leonard's, 98
St Maur, Maj, 10–11
St Pancras Church, 123
St Paul's Cathedral, 17
St Petrock's, 136
St Sidwell's, 38, 92, 138
St Thomas, 17, 20, 32–3, 71, 84, 131
St Thomas Constitutional Club, 50
St Thomas Union, 78
St Thomas Workhouse, 78
Salisbury Plain, 30, 87
Salonica, 106
Salvation Army, 17, 74
Sanders, Charles, 97
Sanders, Mrs, 38
Sandford, Inspector, 53
Sandford, Lt, 121
Sandford Street, 28
Sanger, Lord John, 82–3
Santa Claus ship, 47
Sarajevo, 7
Saskatchewan, 109
Saunders, Pte C., 85
Savile, Col, 97
Savoy, 94
Sayres, Lt-Col, 109
Schrader, Pte Hugo, 132
Scott, Stephen, 134
Serbia, 7, 128–9
Sermon, Mr E.H., 90
Seymour, Mrs Charles, 29
Shakespeare, William, 76

Shear, Spr, 110
Sheldon, Rev'd J.F., 111
Shelley, Sir John, 28
Shobbrook, F.S., 58
Short, C.C., 84
Shortridge, 2nd Cpl E.S., 88
Shute, W.H. Pte, 88
Sidmouth, 55
Sidmouth Garage, 55
Sidwell Street, 10, 113
Silver, Mr C.M., 89
Silverton, 84
Sing, Boys, Sing, 106
Sir Francis Drake bowls team, 25
Skinner, PC, 53
Skinner, Pte, 85
Smart, Pte Albert Edward, 64
Smart Set, The, 74
Smith, Gipsy, 110–11
Smythen Street, 82
Snow, C., 84
Snow, Charles, 58
Snowball, Mr, 99
Socialism, 126
Somerset, 105, 124
Somerset Light Infantry, 38, 40, 105
Somme, Battle of the, 80–1, 86, 96, 114, 128
Sons of the Sea, 134
South African War, 38
Southbrook, 62
Southcott, Pte J., 85
South Devon, 16
Southern Command, 41
Southernhay, 11
Southern League football, 23
Southampton, 84
South of France, 59
South Midland Cyclists, The, 57
South Street, 63

South Western Railway Company, 129
Spiers and Pond, Messrs, 38
Stafford Bridge, 104
Standfield and White, 16, 113
Starcross, 62–3, 85
Stirling, Capt, 120
Stockelle, Violet, 107
Stocker, Mr J., 71, 75, 94, 114
Stokes, James, 79, 103
Stone, C., 84
Stone, Com-Sgt-Maj Albert, 34
Stooker, Mr, 16
Stovell, Col, 90–1
Stowell, Ernest G., 127
Strawbridge, Charles, 90
Streatham Hall Temporary Hospital, 27
Stretcher bearers, 73
Suffolk Regiment, 64
Sugar and Spice, 54
Summer Time Lighting, 102
Sweetie-Sweetie Chorus, 54
Swettenham, Mrs, 108

Talbot, Colonel, 25
Tank Corps, 113
Tank, The, 112–13, 115
Tank Week, 115
Tanner, Miss, 38
Taylor, Cpl Hugh S., 109
Taylor, John, 95
Teignmouth, 101, 108
Ten Tommies, The, 105–106
Terrible, HMS, 119
Territorial RE Drill Hall, 86
Territorials, 8, 13, 24, 26–7, 30, 33–4, 41, 55–6
Theatre Royal, 27, 31, 33, 45, 54, 72, 93–4, 105, 109, 115–16, 133
Thomas, Arthur, 111

Thorne, George, 94
Thorpe Hill, 34
Thought transmission, 95
Thurgood, Lt, 112
Thurgood, Mr and Mrs E.C., 113
Ticket collector, 53
Times, The, 90
Titanic, 25
Tiverton, 74, 85
Tolley, T.D., 84
Tonkin, J.M., 56
Tootell, Pte. Tom, 132
Topsham, 74
Topsham Barracks, 25, 27, 51, 117
Torquay, 59, 85, 124, 135
Torrington, 26
Townhill, PC, 25, 50–1
Tozer, Mr and Mrs, 38
Tramcars, 91
Tram crash, 97
Tregale, Private L., 85
Tremlett, L Cpl W.H., 78
Trenches, 71, 86, 109, 114
Trick, Mr, 78–9
Trump, Thomas, 88
Truro, 56
Turkey, 130
Turks, 128

Union Jack, 77, 136, 138–9
Union of London and Smiths Bank, 97
United States, 98
U.S. Senate, 98

VAD hospitals, 34, 77
VA Hospital, 27, 49, 55, 65, 111
Vakeleich, Michael, 128
Varwell, Mr H.B., 72
Veronique, 25
Victoria Cross, 50, 83

Victoria Hall, 61, 74, 110, 114
Victoria, Queen, 124
Victor Street, 110
Victory War Loan, 113
Vigilancia, 98
Vimy Ridge, 128
Vincent, Mr Bert, 131
Vincent, 2nd-Lt L.A.W., 120, 131
Voluntary Aid Detachment, 42
Volunteer Force, 52–3, 57, 79, 95

Walsh, Col, 68
Walton and Co, Messrs., 138
Waratahs, The, 125
War Bonds, 112–13, 115
War Book of Facts, 18–19
War Economy Campaign, 112
War-eye, 61
Ward, Bombardier A., 34
Ward, Sgtt-Maj, 34
War Office, 28, 52, 63, 69, 95, 107
War Seal Foundation, 107
Warwickshire Yeomanry, 77
Waterloo, Battle of, 17
Webber, Messrs J., 89
Webber, Mr, 119
Webb, Rev S.L., 88
Wedlake, Pte G., 85
Weeks, PC, 51
Welchman, Rev'd H. de Vere, 85–6, 98, 100
Wellington, 56
Wessex Brigade, RFA, 62
Wessex Division of the Royal Field Artillery, 25
Wessex RAMC, 109
Western, Col, 41
Western Counties Institution, 63
Western Front, 78, 83, 87, 96, 102, 109–10, 112, 114–15, 120, 124, 126, 128, 130, 132–4

West Ham, 23
West of England Eye Hospital, 27, 60
Westron, Miss Francis Althea, 123
What Money Can't Buy, 125
White, Sgt G.T., 41
Whit-Monday military sports, 58
Widgery, Jack, 83–4
Willey and Co, Messrs, 55
Willey's Avenue, 103
William IV, 124
Williams, Pte A.H., 88
Wilson, President, 98, 133
Wilts Regiment, 67–8
Windsor Castle, 96
Winnipeg, 109
Winter, Pte, 85
Wissman, Lt, 25
Withycombe, 78
Witt, Paul, 125
Woking, 130
Wolseley, Vicountess, 54
Wolvercote, 109
Women and the War, 134
Wonderful Wessex, 81
Wonford, 25, 62
Wood, Mr F.W., 58
Woodbury, 8–9, 30
Woodford, 66
Woodward, Pte Edward Harold, 105
Woolwich, 51
Woore, Dr, 90
Worcestershire Regiment, 112
Workhouse, 78–80
Wotton, Pte Thomas, 126
Wray, Maj, 126
Wreford, P.S., 95
Wynter, Major H.T., 25

Yellowstone News, 98

Yeomanry, 10–11, 28, 77
York Road, 11
Yorkshire Regiment, 120
Young Men's Christian Association
    (YMCA), 30, 110–11, 125–6
Ypres, 34–5, 110

Zeebrugge, 121–2
Zeppelin, 51–2, 75